Win-Win Agile Games

Trusted Teams For Improved Results

SAVITHA KATHAM

Win-Win Agile Games. Trusted teams for improved results.

Savitha Katham

Win-Win Agile Games: Trusted Teams For Improved Results.
First edition October, 2019

Published by:
Phenom Books LLC
PO Box 160, N Billerica,
MA – 01862
phenombooksllc@gmail.com

ISBN: 978-1-7339780-0-2

This work is licensed under a Creative Commons Attribution-ShareAlike 4.0 International License.

Win-Win Agile Games. Trusted teams for improved results.

DISCLAIMER

All content contained in this book is for informational and educational purposes only. The author is not in any way accountable for any results or outcomes that occur because of using this material. Constructive attempts have been made to provide information that is both accurate and effective, but the author is not bound by the accuracy or use/misuse of this information. Any situation mentioned in this book or resemblance to any organization is purely coincidental.

Win-Win Agile Games. Trusted teams for improved results.

I dedicate this book at the divine feet of
Baba, Guruji, and Mom.

Win-Win Agile Games. Trusted teams for improved results.

ACKNOWLEDGMENTS

Thanks to everyone who inspired me directly and indirectly. Special thanks to mentor Rich, editors Hillary and Jen and illustrator Rafael for partnering with me throughout this writing journey. I want to thank Agile communities, peer agilistas, and everyone who made a positive impact on me and helped me to write this book.

Win-Win Agile Games. Trusted teams for improved results.

CONTENTS

Foreword 1

Preface 7

Game Preparation 9

    Process And Steps 10

Pre-Read 15

Estimation Games 17

    Affinity Estimation 18

    Relative Sizing: Fibonacci 22

    Poker Estimation 26

    Lean Penny Game 31

Scoping Games 35

    Paper Airplane 36

    Classify Features 44

    Definition Of Out And Ready (Door) 48

    Empathy Map 53

    Effective Teams 57

    Forced Ranking 62

    Kano Model 66

    Prune The Product Tree 70

    Dot Voting 75

    Open Space 79

Win-Win Agile Games. Trusted teams for improved results.

Retrospective Games 85

    Secret Pot 86

    Sailboat 90

    Memory Tester 94

    Pechakucha 97

Communication Games 101

    Squaring The Circle 102

    Blind Drawing 106

    Lost In Translation 110

    Rope Nope 114

    I, You, We 118

    Agile Bingo 122

    I And I (Incremental And Iterative) 126

    Innovate 130

    Conflict Gone 134

Icebreaker Games 138

    Human Knot 139

    Know Them 143

    ESVP 146

    Helium Stick 150

    Help! Help! 154

References 159

[This page is intentionally left blank.]

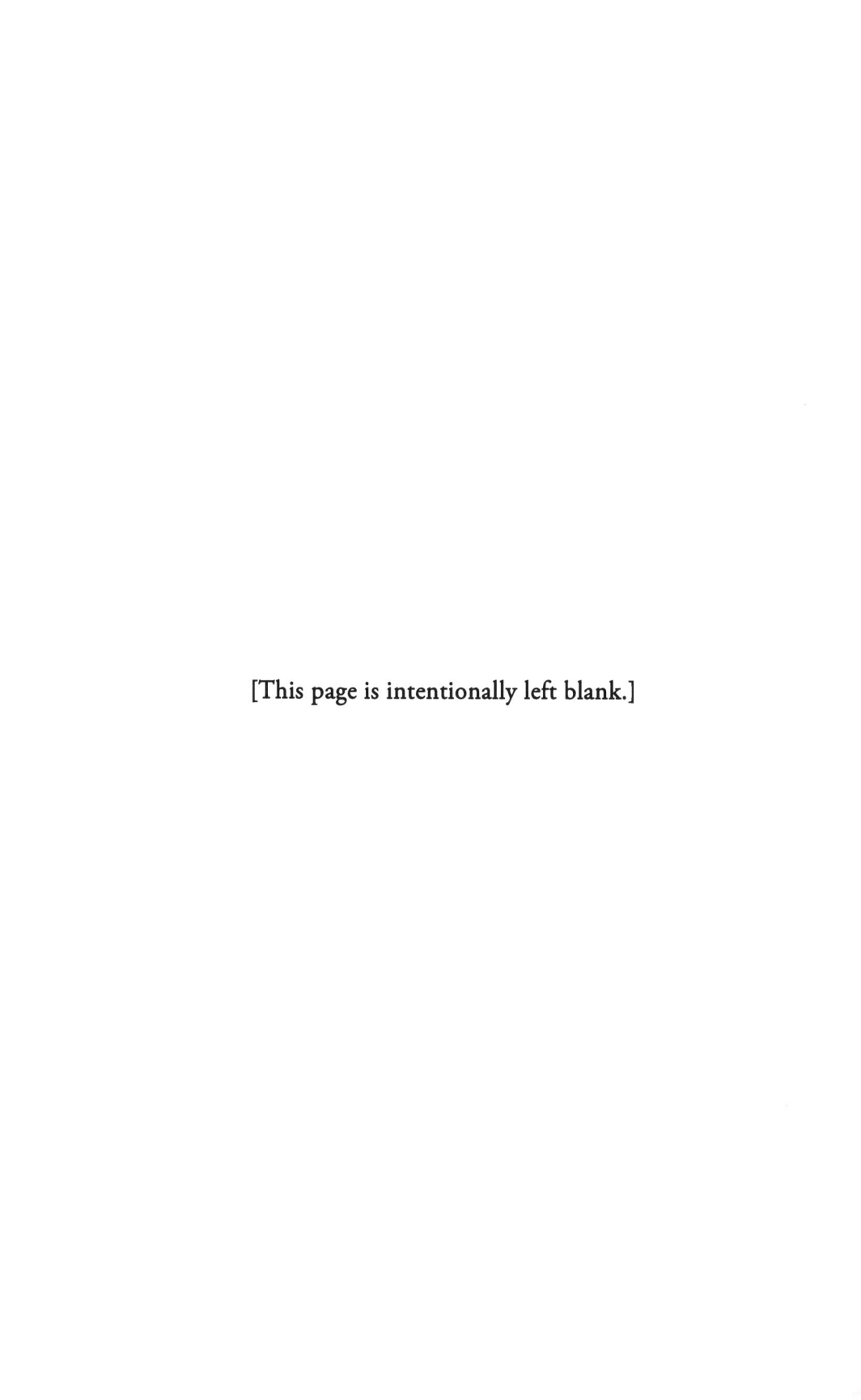

FOREWORD

―――●・・●・・●―――

Agile Games — the power of simplicity

I was thrilled when Savvy asked me to write a forward for her book on agile games! This work will be of great value to agilists everywhere, and indeed to trainers and facilitators in any industry where people work together in teams to get things done.

I am the current president of Agile New England. We proudly host the global Agile Games Conference every year, right here in Boston. These activities have the power to transform the way we collaborate — a power sometimes disguised by their simplicity. As with all things agile, the magic is setting your intentions and reflecting on your results. Win-Win Agile Games will help you harness the power of playfulness for your teams.

It seems like every team leader or facilitator has used playful activities at some point to help their teams to bond, to work together towards some common outcome. Our work culture is littered with stories of throwing eggs off of buildings or constructing towers from spaghetti and marshmallows. Anything that helps us align and collaborate is positive. However, when games are designed to teach and reinforce specific agile principles, that's when the learning is 10xed — and team performance is similarly enhanced.

Take the utter simplicity of the Ball Point Game:

All you need is a small bag of balls (I use soft foam practice golf balls) — no pasta or sugar are hurt in this exercise. The aim is to score points as a team. This is a co-operative, rather than competitive, activity. You earn a point every time you collectively take a ball out of the bag, do something with it, and then put it back in the bag. (I told you it was simple.)

Of course, there are additional rules, the constraints that make the game interesting — such as "everyone on the team has to touch the ball exactly once," "no points for a dropped ball," and "you can't pass the ball to someone adjacent to you." You play the game for two minutes, then talk to each other for one minute. And then you do it again.

If all you did was to play this game as a fun team-building activity, it would work. You would benefit from it. Playing cooperatively, with time pressure, creates a playful way to support each other and collaborate towards a shared outcome. You'd probably get bored after a few rounds, but a smart facilitator would intervene before that point. You could then embark on your real work more successfully, having reduced any tension or boredom and unleashed a bit more energy in the team.

But don't forget the debrief! Debriefing is how we unleash the power of a game like this. Spend some time after the activity talking about it with each other, reflecting on what we noticed and what we learned. For example:

- Forecasting — you use iterative feedback after each round to try to forecast your score in the next one. Is the team improving? What effect does having a forecast have on the deliverable? How did you come up with the first forecast? After your initial wild guess (let's be honest about that initial forecast), were your subsequent forecasts better? Did you score more points just from getting more practice? We can learn a lot about when and how to make forecasts for real work projects. (Hint: if you want good forecasts, do it iteratively in small chunks. If you want bad forecasts, do it at the beginning of a large project, when you know the least about the work you're about to start together.)

- What about Priming Bias? Do we get anchored when the highest-authority person in the room tells you what your score should be? How much does the so-called expert's advice constrain the team? What happens we a cheeky trainer tells them about a fabricated "world record for teams of your size," and it's off the charts? The intersection of expectation and motivation is always ripe for learning and exploration.

- What about the accuracy of the team's forecasts? What if the team got a bonus for hitting their forecast or a penalty for missing it? Are we go-getters, always trying to beat our forecast, or do we start to take it easy as we get closer to our goal?

- What if someone played the role, "facilitator," and watched the rest of the team as they did the work? What happens when one person guides and shapes the work rather than doing it with the rest of the team? Is that how a Scrum Master might help a real work team? Would that make it easier for everybody to concentrate on their own part in the activity? How would it affect individual ownership of group success?

- Can efficiency — and therefore, the outcome — be improved by specializing roles in some way? For example, one person holds the bag, another takes balls out, a third puts the balls in… Who decides who will be best at which role? Are some roles more fun or more intrinsically motivating than others?

- What about diversity and inclusion? What are the diversity dimensions that matter? Hand size, height, and clumsiness are obvious ones in this game. Did gender play any role in how the team interacted? Did we go out of our way to include everyone's ideas and skills in the team's success?

- Does anyone dislike or avoid playing games? Were they courageous enough to pass or check out? Could they still be helpful as an outside observer?

- What happens when, inevitably, someone drops the ball? How does the team react? How does this affect how people play the game in future iterations, regardless of who let it slip? What does the team learn about itself from dissecting the experience at the end of the round? What can they do differently as a team next time?
- Is there anything about this game that is like your real everyday work?

And, of course, the iterative process that we used to play the game — make a plan together, do the activity together, reflect, and repeat — it turns out it's a great way to work, and we'll probably try it with our real work.

Playing a game like this is the perfect introduction to agile software development. It's just as good face-to-face as it is online. With the help of the global Agile Games community, we've created a variation of the game that can be played entirely online using Trello. (There's not quite as much laughter and energy, but it still brings out all the learning points.)

The games in this book work. They are simple and powerful. You can use them as the basis for creating your own learning tools, as well as for helping your teams get their real work done.

For example, to harness the collective intelligence of the team to make good estimates and forecasts, Savvy shares ideas like Affinity Estimation,

Win-Win Agile Games. Trusted teams for improved results.

Relative Sizing: Fibonacci, and Poker Estimation. Each one addresses a slightly different challenge your team might be facing in their empirical planning process — different cognitive biases, issues with the application of the Scrum framework, failure to work effectively with complexity, inability to see things from another person's point of view, and so on.

And each of the games can be further adapted, like a base recipe into which you can add your favorite flavors. You can return to them again and again. You can build upon them as your team develops and grows together — facing new challenges in new creative ways.

Adapting, sharing, learning, and doing: these are the ingredients of successful learning and successful teamwork. This book will give you everything you need to steadily grow your go-to toolset of agile games, as you incorporate them into your regular practice.

Enjoy!

Richard Kasperowski

Author, teacher, speaker, and coach
President, Agile New England
www.kasperowski.com
Boston, Massachusetts
October 29, 2019

PREFACE

People usually prefer informal, relaxed environments such as a party at a friend's place, or a three-day workshop at a workplace. Informal settings help people to open up. They also trigger mental relaxation, which resets creative juices and allows for greater participation.

As an executive coach, I have used games as a means to elicit involvement from my clients. Games bring out people's real personalities, build trust, help them to speak up about challenges, and facilitate successful collaboration.

The word "game" has different meanings to different people. Games are not always for entertainment. Outcome-based games, a term I coined, are played with a specific agenda in mind. Detailed planning and preparations are required to execute these games well and make them worth the attendees' time. Essentially, time is money in the case of these games. All the participation time attendees put in can be translated into money. So it is essential that these games are played correctly.

This book contains a collection of games I have played with my clients and customers during various engagements. I have learned—and customized—these games based on reading books; participating in training sessions, conferences, or conventions; and through speaking with industry peers and conducting research online. I am publishing this book so coaches can access essential games in one place.

With so many books on Agile games, why another? My aim in writing this book is to pay forward what I have learned. This book can serve as a great start to step into consulting engagements. Outcome-based games challenge our creativity and test our ability to think outside the box. Although this book demonstrates specific ways to conduct games, it doesn't stop facilitators from customizing them to meet their needs. Read each game as a reference and feel free to add your flavor to make it more personable.

I have tried to mention the sources or author's names for each game when I could locate that information. Of course, I wish to give credit for the games wherever possible, so if you know the authors or inventors of any of the games whose names have not been mentioned, please do email me. I would be happy to mention their names in future editions of this book.

> "I hope you find games in this book that touch your heart and your art."

Books are portable chips for the future. Humankind may write history, but books live on!

Thanks for holding this book in your hands!

Sincerely,
Savitha Katham

Win-Win Agile Games. Trusted teams for improved results.

GAME PREPARATION

Win-Win Agile Games. Trusted teams for improved results.

PROCESS AND STEPS

Game Preparation, Processes, and Steps

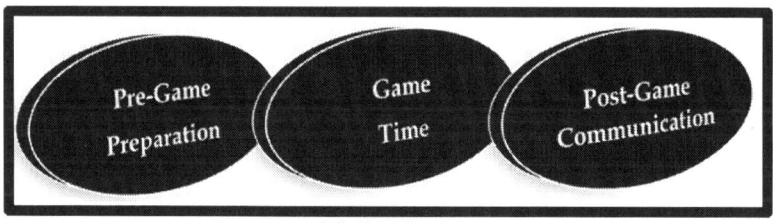

PC: Game Steps

What are the Outcome-Based Games?

- Outcome-based games encompass activities, exercises, and workshops played with a specific outcome in mind for a targeted audience within an organization.

- Outcome-based games are team-based and require collaboration, involvement, and team energy. I have yet to hear of these games being played solo while still achieving the expected results.

Why Play These Games?

- The short answer is to find a solution to a specific problem statement, situation, or activity.

- The long answer is to address various situations, challenges, opportunities, and problems. For example, these games may be played to increase team-building and bonding, consolidate innovative ideas, learn more about a framework and its delivery, focus on management problems and decision-making, spread awareness about a change, find solutions to customer problems, develop client relationships, or increase sales.
- These games provide avenues to help identify problems and inspire the right solutions for internal or external customers.
- Playing creates a safe environment for team members to express themselves without fear.
- The game environment brings impediments to light and offers continuous feedback and improvement.
- These games offer a stage to give birth to innovative ideas.
- These games are played in an informal environment to bring to light weaknesses and threats and address them through strengths and opportunities.

The Four W's and the H of Playing These Games

When?

- Play these games when you have a topic of interest (i.e., problem) along with detailed agenda and outcomes of the game
- Ask yourself: What do you want to solve or create today?

- ❏ A more magnificent team?
- ❏ An innovative idea?
- ❏ Improved delivery?
- ❏ A leader 2.0?

Why?

- To generate solutions.

Who?

- Decide who should attend.
- Consolidate the list of attendees.
- Understand timing constraints.
- Decide whether the game will be played in person or as an online activity.

Where?

- Finalize logistics: date, time, location, and so on.
- Accommodate the needs of the game.
  - ❏ Will it be held outdoors or indoors?
  - ❏ Some participants cannot perform certain physical activities. Check with attendees to determine additional requirements.
  - ❏ If hosting an indoor activity, reserve the conference room. If team members are traveling, plan for accommodations in advance.

- Identify a location where it is conducive for teams to play the game.
- Discuss attendees' availability before finalizing game dates.
- Consider:
  - ❑ Food
  - ❑ Stationery
  - ❑ Props
  - ❑ Furniture
  - ❑ How to aim for maximum participation to make the games as successful as possible.

How?

- Form a game-planning champions team and communicate the roles well in advance to all participants. These are the people who will be on the team.
  - ❑ **Organizer:** Oversees the management of the game from start to finish.
  - ❑ **Coordinator:** Coordinates the logistics and communication about the game.
  - ❑ **Facilitator:** Facilitates the game on the day of the event.
  - ❑ **Attendees or Teams:** Participants in the game.
- Key Points
  - ❑ Select appropriate games to increase the success of the expected outcome.

- ☐ Print paperwork in advance.
- ☐ Have a backup plan for last-minute no-shows.
- ☐ Rehearse the game with a small set of people, if possible, in advance.
- ☐ Document the outcomes.
- ☐ Create an action-item list and assign owners and dates.
- ☐ Monitor and complete the action items.
- ☐ Close the problem when expected results are achieved.
- ☐ If expected results are not achieved, pursue other alternative options to mitigate the problem.
- Will the games be open-ended or closed-ended?
  - ☐ Open-ended games result in a higher number of ideas and an overflow of creative energy.
  - ☐ Closed-ended games end quickly as soon as a specific answer is given or the result is achieved.

Post-game: Next steps
- Survey to seek feedback.
- Incorporate suggestions into the next game event.

Win-Win Agile Games. Trusted teams for improved results.

PRE-READ

Agile term	Generic term
Scrum master	Project manager, project lead, manager
Product owner	Business lead, business manager, business subject matter expert
SME (subject matter expert)	Experienced professionals with knowledge in a specific product or technology
Product backlog	Business requirements document
Scrum team	The project team (For example, developers, test lead, tech lead, and testers). If you are a non-IT group, use your existing roles to call as a Scrum team
Retrospectives	Lessons learned ceremony
Epics	A business requirement at the 30,000-foot level with a high degree of uncertainty and risk
Features	A business requirement for a specific functionality or a module
User story	The smallest level of business requirement with a high rate of accuracy where teams can understand for implementation
Sprint or iteration	Timeboxed event that starts and ends within a specified duration
WIP (work in progress)	A batch of work that's in progress
Definition of ready	A business requirement is clearly stated for the teams to work on (for example, to code or to test)

Definition of done	A business requirement is complete as per the acceptance criteria
Kanban	Visual representation of work on a board—physical or online
QA Lead	Quality Assurance Lead
Timebox	Fixed time limits within which planned game, or a specific round of a game is completed
POC	Proof of concept *"Realization of a certain method or idea to demonstrate its feasibility, [or a demonstration in principle with the aim of verifying that some concept or theory has practical potential." (Source: Wikipedia)*
Greenfield project	A new project with no dependency on existing systems or applications *"…In software development, a greenfield project could be one of developing a system for a totally new environment, without concern for integrating with other systems, especially not legacy systems." (Source: Wikipedia)*
[Meeting] Parking lot	Collection of items that need additional discussions at a later time and are not specific to the current meeting. This list is tracked to keep the current meeting on-track without any digression

Win-Win Agile Games. Trusted teams for improved results.

ESTIMATION GAMES

Win-Win Agile Games. Trusted teams for improved results.

AFFINITY ESTIMATION

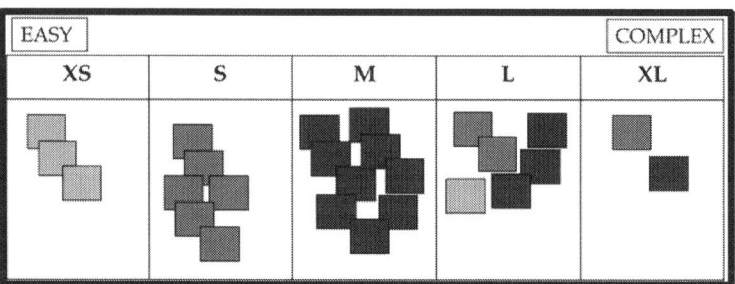

PC: Affinity Estimation

- **Game Categories:**

| Team Building | Professional Coaching | Retrospectives | Leadership | Others |

- **Game Name:** Affinity Estimation

- **Objective:** Play this game to size the product backlog. Estimation exercises help to reach a common consensus and encourage involvement from team members. Affinity Estimation increases the participant's level of understanding and initial estimates (relative sizing) and documenting assumptions and risks (to address variability).

- **Facilitator:** A coach, trainer, or Scrum master.

- **Suggested Attendees:** Product owners, subject matter experts (SMEs), tech leads, enterprise architect, Quality Assurance leads, and Scrum team(s).

- **Required Materials:** Conference room, pens, and papers.

- **Prerequisites:**
  - List of features or user stories for discussion.
  - T-shirt size buckets from XS, S, M, L, XL where the smallest size (XS) is "easy" and the largest size (XL) is "complex".
  - Estimation size buckets pasted on the wall so attendees can place the features or user stories under the respective bucket.
  - Set up a flip chart paper to track parking lot items.

- **Instructions:**
  - Round 1
    - All team members line up.
    - Each team member picks a feature or user story and places it under the respective estimation bucket based on their experience and understanding. This activity is repeated until all features or user stories are complete.
      - This step is done in silence. Team members are not allowed to talk to each other.
      - Vague user stories are placed in the parking lot for detailed discussions later.
  - Round 2
    - All team members reconvene to review sizing estimates together. Team members discuss estimates and re-bucket the stories if required.

- ❑ If a feature is classified as M in round 1, in round 2 it can be moved to another bucket based on the team discussions.
- ❑ Teams are encouraged to break down user stories that are in XL bucket into smaller, logical features or user stories for more clarity.

- **Timing:**
  - ❑ 45–60 minutes
    - ❑ Introduction: 5–10 minutes
    - ❑ Round 1: 10–15 minutes
    - ❑ Round 2: 10–15 minutes
    - ❑ Debrief: Remaining time

- **Suggested questions for debriefing:**
  - ❑ What did team members think of silent estimation?
  - ❑ Did any team members collaborate with signals during round 1?
  - ❑ Was there a high consensus rate in round 1 or round 2?
  - ❑ What did the team learn from this exercise?
  - ❑ How is this game different from other estimation games (if teams are played any before)?

- **Variations:**
  - ❑ Play with established Scrum teams for backlog creation and refinement, relative sizing of features, and to understand the complexity of the backlog.

- **Tips and Tricks:**
  - ❑ The Facilitators are encouraged to try variations of this game.

- **Reader Notes:** (Write possible variations and notes below.)
  - ❑ _____
  - ❑ _____
  - ❑ _____

- **Best Time to Play:**

KICK-OFF	PLAN	DO	CHECK	ADJUST
Initiate	*Plan*	*Perform*	*Monitor*	*Improve*

- **Source:** Unknown.

- **Author Notes:** I learned about this game during an Agile training session. Because it is quick and easy to play, I instantly connected with it. Within a relatively short period of time, team members came together to move the features or user stories to the right buckets, and then have productive conversations that resulted in identifying additional requirements.

Win-Win Agile Games. Trusted teams for improved results.

RELATIVE SIZING: FIBONACCI

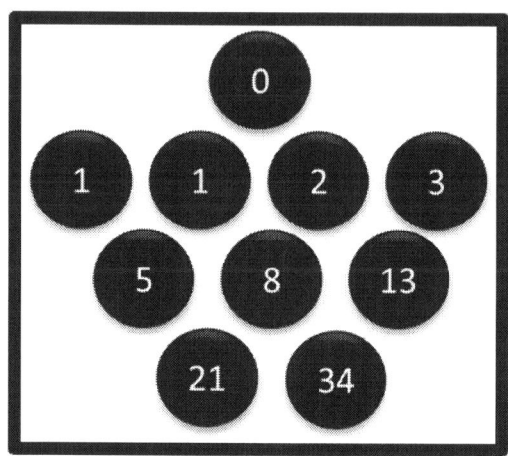

PC: Relative sizing: Fibonacci

- **Game Categories:**

Team Building	Professional Coaching	Retrospectives	Leadership	Others

- **Game Name:** Relative Sizing: Fibonacci
- **Objective:** Play this game to get teams to understand their collective efforts in achieving adequate estimations. This game highlights group understanding over individual experience.
- **Facilitator:** A coach, trainer, or Scrum master.
- **Suggested Attendees:** Scrum team(s).
- **Required Materials:** Conference room, sticky notes, pens, and pictures (animals, buildings, or mixed images).

- **Prerequisites:** Logistics planning.
- **Instructions:**
  - Round 1 – individual estimation (no group)
    - Facilitator assigns each attendee a Fibonacci number: 1, 1, 2, 3, 5, 8, 11, 13, where 1 is the smallest effort and 13 is the most complex effort.
    - Facilitator shows a picture (for example, a banyan tree) and asks attendees to size the picture and write the sizing on a sticky note—without discussing the estimates with others.
    - On the count of three, all attendees show their numbers.
    - Ask the lowest and highest sizing team members to come forward and explain the rationale behind their numbers.
  - Round 2 – estimation with a team of two
    - Form groups of two people.
    - Show the same picture again and ask attendees to size the picture.
    - Ask teams to document the assumptions for the numbers.
    - Discuss with teams the difference in sizing from round 1 to 2.
    - Ask what has changed and what they have learned.
  - Round 3 – estimation as a group
    - Ask attendees to form groups of five to eight people.

- ❑ Show another picture (for example, a lion) to all teams and ask attendees to size the picture by documenting their assumptions (understanding).
- ❑ Discuss with the teams the difference in sizing from rounds 1, 2, and 3.
- ❑ Ask what has changed and what they have learned.

- **Timing:**
  - ❑ 30-45 minutes
    - ❑ Game: 25-30 minutes
    - ❑ Debrief: Remaining time

- **Suggested questions for debriefing:**
  - ❑ What did teams learn from individual versus group sizing estimates?
  - ❑ What risks did teams identify?
  - ❑ Were requirements clear from the Product owner?
  - ❑ Did teams have the right expertise to estimate?
  - ❑ Did team members collaborate while discussing the assumptions?
  - ❑ Did teams identify any dependencies between one another? If yes, how are these dependencies handled by teams?

- **Variations:**
  - ❑ The Facilitators are encouraged to try variations of this game.
  - ❑ The number of rounds can be reduced if teams are small.

❏ Encourage teams to interact with one another.

- **Tips and Tricks:**
  ❏ Consider small prizes for the winning team.

- **Reader Notes:** (Write possible variations and notes below.)
  ❏ _____
  ❏ _____
  ❏ _____

- **Best Time to Play:**

KICK-OFF	PLAN	DO	CHECK	ADJUST
Initiate	*Plan*	*Perform*	*Monitor*	*Improve*

- **Source:** Unknown.

- **Author Notes:** In many traditional estimation practices, a tech lead or project manager gives an estimate on behalf of team members. In contrast, this game brings a sense of empowerment and inclusion to the team. It results in increased participation and better estimation as a group because they feel a sense of ownership regarding delivery.

POKER ESTIMATION

PC: Poker Estimation

- **Game Categories:**

Team Building	Professional Coaching	Retrospectives	Leadership	Others

- **Game Name:** Poker Estimation
- **Objective:** Play this game to help teams understand the complexity of items in the product backlog.
- **Facilitator:** A coach, trainer, or Scrum master.
- **Suggested Attendees:** Product owner, subject matter experts (SMEs), Quality Assurance lead, architect, and tech lead.

- **Required Materials:** Conference room, the product backlog with prioritized user stories, and poker cards or sheets of paper containing Fibonacci numbers from 1 to 13: 1, 1, 2, 3, 5, 8, 13.

- **Prerequisites:**
  - ❏ The entire team must have the latest copy of the product backlog with the top 10 prioritized user stories.
  - ❏ Known dependencies must be identified before the game.
  - ❏ Fibonacci sequence numbers are written on sticky notes or on printed cards (poker cards).

- **Instructions:**
  - ❏ Form groups of seven to nine people.
  - ❏ The facilitator provides details on how to use the Fibonacci series:
    - ❏ Numbers up to 5 are the smallest sizes, numbers between 5 and 8 are medium size, and numbers above 8 are large in size.
    - ❏ Do not go beyond 13 to reduce the risk of estimation challenges and size disparities. If any user story is larger than 13, split the story into smaller stories and reestimate.
  - ❏ Teams are given a set of numbered cards or sheets of paper.
  - ❏ The facilitator reads the description of the user story aloud, and the participating team members are asked to estimate the size of the user story based on their experience and knowledge. Team

members may discuss their assumptions before providing the relative size estimations.
- ❏ When requested, all team members show their estimation cards simultaneously. Fibonacci numbers are exponential, not linear. Teams can easily understand how the level of accuracy is fading as they pick large numbers in the series. The higher the number in the series showing increased uncertainty, risk and complexity.
- ❏ A discussion should be encouraged if the estimates have a considerable gap. All team members need to agree on a median number.
- ❏ If the selected estimate numbers by all team members have a low gap, then the team decides to choose the commonly agreed-upon number.
- ❏ For example, if four team members display 1, 3, 5, and 8, then the team discusses whether they will use the average number or the higher number.
- ❏ SMEs can clarify the assumptions behind selecting the high numbers, and brainstorm until everyone agrees on the size of the story.

- **Timing:**
    - ❏ 60–120 minutes, depending on the number of user stories
        - ❏ Introduction: 5–10 minutes
        - ❏ Game: Remaining time

- **Debriefing:**
  - ❏ What did teams learn from this exercise?
  - ❏ Did any role try estimating for other roles (or on behalf of another role)?
  - ❏ What can teams take away from brainstorming?

- **Variations:**
  - ❏ Teams can shout out their estimation numbers or write them on a sticky note to show to others.
  - ❏ Use online poker tools.

- **Tips and Tricks:**
  - ❏ The Facilitators are encouraged to try variations of this game.
  - ❏ Team members can consult or talk to peers before finalizing their sizing numbers.
  - ❏ Timebox the activity so that all user stories are covered.

- **Reader Notes:** (Write possible variations and notes below.)
  - ❏ _____
  - ❏ _____
  - ❏ _____

- **Best Time to Play:**

KICK-OFF	PLAN	DO	CHECK	ADJUST
Initiate	*Plan*	*Perform*	*Monitor*	*Improve*

- **Source:** Unknown.

- **Author Notes:** What I like about this game is the difference of opinions that are shared in a constructive manner. This game dispels any assumptions or biases around any particular role in a team. All roles—developers, testers, architects, and business analysts—are given equal importance while estimating the user stories. During earlier coaching days when Agile was still new, one tester came to me and said, "I didn't know testers could provide estimates, too!" I smiled and said, "Not just testers. All roles get to collaborate in the estimation." Attendees' reactions and feedback reconfirm how powerful these games are in bringing out the right culture and recognizing everyone's contributions in appropriately sizing user stories for predictable delivery.

Win-Win Agile Games. Trusted teams for improved results.

LEAN PENNY GAME

PC: Lean Penny Game

- **Game Categories:**

| Team Building | Professional Coaching | Retrospectives | Leadership | Others |

- **Game Name:** Lean Penny Game
- **Objective:** Play this game to (a) understand Lean concepts like small versus large batches and sufficient work pull, and to (b) create productive teams.
- **Facilitator:** A coach, trainer, or Scrum master.
- **Suggested Attendees:** Product owner, and Scrum team(s).
- **Required Materials:** Conference room, and 50–75 pennies (or more, depending on attendee count).
- **Prerequisites:** Logistics planning.
- **Instructions:**

- Form equal groups of four to six people.
- Round 1
  - Timebox: 50 seconds.
  - Each team gets 10-15 coins. Each team should have the same number of coins.
  - When the timer starts, the first member of each team flips all 15 coins in the air one at a time and then passes all the coins to the next team member, who also flips them. The coins are passed to all team members in sequence. The last person should keep the coins after flipping.
  - Any coins that have been flipped by any person at the end of the 50 seconds are considered in progress. Coins that have been flipped by each person are counted as completed work.
  - The team which flips and completes the most coins within the time limit wins.
- Round 2
  - Timebox: 50 seconds.
  - Each team gets 10–15 coins. Each team should have the same number of coins.
  - When the timer starts, the first member of each team flips all 15 coins in the air one at a time and then passes each set of coins to the next team member, who also flips them. The coins are passed to all team members in sequence. The last person should keep the coins after flipping.

- At any given time, each team member should have only three coins to flip (limit the work).
- Teams can reuse the coins to continue the game if there's any time left. For example, if the first person does not have any coins to flip, he or she can take coins from the last person and continue the game.
- Each batch is completed when all three coins have been flipped by all team members.
- The team that has completed the highest number of batches (one batch is three coins) is the winner for the round.
- The objective of this game is to help teams understand the benefit of small batches of work. Small batches help to complete the work faster and make teams more engaged and productive; large batches tend to have inconsistent workloads resulting in not using the team's efficiency to the maximum extent.

- **Suggested questions for debriefing:**
  - What differences have team members seen from round 1 to round 2?
  - What has changed in round 2?
  - Which round had more work in progress?
  - What were other team members doing in round 1 while the first person was flipping the coins?

- **Tips and Tricks:**
  - ❑ The Facilitators are encouraged to try variations of this game.
  - ❑ Add a third round (#3) and ask teams to flip one coin at a time and pass it to the next team member.
- **Reader Notes:** (Write possible variations and notes below.)
  - ❑ _____
  - ❑ _____
  - ❑ _____
- **Best Time to Play:**

KICK-OFF	PLAN	DO	CHECK	ADJUST
Initiate	*Plan*	*Perform*	*Monitor*	*Improve*

- **Source:** Unknown.
- **Author Notes:** This is my go-to game for my Agile elevator pitch to management. It is very powerful, and I look forward to the debriefing. It is very interesting to learn what management gets out of this game. It's is a winner in getting management's attention on transformation.

Win-Win Agile Games. Trusted teams for improved results.

SCOPING GAMES

Win-Win Agile Games. Trusted teams for improved results.

PAPER AIRPLANE

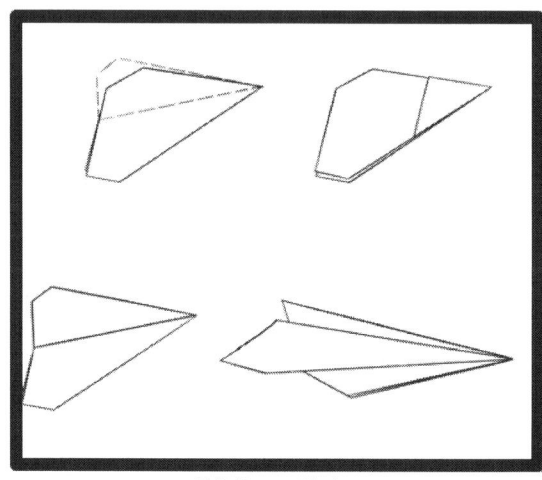

PC: *Paper Airplane*

- **Game Categories:**

| Team Building | Professional Coaching | Retrospectives | Leadership | Others |

- **Game Name:** Paper Airplane
- **Objective:** Play this game to build team interactions with focused delivery. Understanding the requirements to develop a plane per the customer's requirements is the singular goal for all participants.
- **Facilitator:** A coach, trainer, or Scrum master.
- **Suggested Attendees:** Product owners, and Scrum team(s).
- **Required Materials:** Conference Room, flip chart, and one to two bundles of A4 paper.

Win-Win Agile Games. Trusted teams for improved results.

- **Prerequisites:**
  - ❑ Create three columns on the flip chart: 1) forecast number 2) actual number, and 3) wastage. Wastage is defined as an airplane that cannot fly per the requirements (paper wastage).

- **Instructions:**
  - ❑ Form groups of four to six people.
  - ❑ Round 1: <u>Business role only</u>
    - ❑ Facilitator creates three columns on the flip chart: forecast number, actual number, and wastage.
    - ❑ Each group should assign a business role to one person. The business role will provide the requirements for creating a paper airplane.
    - ❑ The facilitator gives just one initial direction to all business roles "The customer needs airplanes." The facilitator does not show the picture of the customer's airplane or demonstrate how to build an airplane. No additional information is given unless questions are asked by a member of a team.
    - ❑ The facilitator can expect questions such as:
      - ❑ What kind of airplane shape and size does the customer want?
      - ❑ How far should it fly? (Example: 5–10 meters.)
      - ❑ How many airplanes are needed?

- Will you be okay approving the proof of concept (POC) in the first sprint and production starting after approval?
- Each business role takes the requirements back to their team.
- The facilitator asks each team how many airplanes they can create in two minutes and writes the number from each team in the forecast number column on the flip chart. Upon completion of the round, forecast versus actual numbers is compared for debriefing.
- Round 1 observations:
  - Expect different shapes and sizes of airplanes due to no synchronization or understanding of the product.
  - Everybody on the team will be creating airplanes with no role clarity.
  - Lots of wastage will likely occur due to no emphasis on quality, understanding of what is being developed, or clear vision and communication.
- Round 2: Role definition and no work in progress (WIP) limit; change of instructions
  - Each group should identify roles, and each role should do only their job; for example, the business role provides the requirements, the developer folds the paper to make

the airplanes, the tester does quality assurance, and so on.
- ❏ The facilitator can expect questions from the business such as:
- ❏ How far should the airplane fly?
- ❏ Each business role takes the requirements back to their teams.
- ❏ The facilitator asks each team how many airplanes they can create in two minutes and writes forecast numbers on a flip chart.
- ❏ Upon completion of the round, forecast versus actual numbers is compared for debriefing.
- ❏ Round 2 observations:
  - ❏ Expect the same shapes of airplanes, and a high success rate as specific roles are appointed to specific activities.
  - ❏ All team members are doing their job based on their roles.
  - ❏ Expect teams to share their different experiences in helping others in their roles.
  - ❏ Expect wastage in the form of half-done airplanes.
- ❏ Round 3: Role definition and set WIP limit; change of instructions
  - ❏ Each group should identify roles, and each role should do only their job; for example, the business role provides

the requirements, the developer folds the papers to make the airplane, the tester does testing, and so on.
- ❑ Each business role takes the requirements back to their teams.
- ❑ Each role has a limit of four papers to make planes. Team members cannot pick up another set of four papers until they move the current set to the next person. For example, a developer should fold four papers at a time and wait until those are given to the next team member before working on the next set of four papers.
- ❑ With every team member working with a four-paper batch, the aim is to achieve a WIP limit for each team member or role.
- ❑ The facilitator asks each team how many airplanes they can create in two minutes and writes down the forecast from each team on a flip chart.
- ❑ Upon completion of the round, forecast versus actual numbers is compared for debriefing.
- ❑ Round 3 observations:
  - ❑ Expect the same shapes of airplanes.
  - ❑ Expect reduced wastage than in round 2 due to WIP limits.

- **Timing:**
  - ❑ 60–75 minutes, depending upon the number of rounds played
    - ❑ Round 1: 5–10 minutes

- ☐ Round 2: 5–10 minutes
- ☐ Round 3: 5–10 minutes
- ☐ Debrief: Remaining time

- **Suggested questions for debriefing:**
- ☐ Round 1:
    - ☐ Did the team understand the vision of the product?
    - ☐ Did anyone ask how far the airplane should fly?
    - ☐ Did the team try seeking business approval for the first airplane before moving on and creating multiple airplanes?
    - ☐ Did anyone confirm the acceptance criteria with the Product owner?
    - ☐ Was any testing done on the flying?
    - ☐ How much [paper] wastage was produced per team? What are the reasons for the wastage?
    - ☐ Did any team take on roles even though the facilitator specified there would be no roles in round 1?
    - ☐ What did teams do differently from round 1 to round 2?
    - ☐ Did teams take the time to discuss the product?
    - ☐ What steps did teams take to avoid [paper] wastage?
- ☐ Round 2:
    - ☐ How does role clarity help?
    - ☐ How does assigning roles help in the delivery?

- What else did the teams learn from the previous round? Did they try to implement new methods/processes/strategies/tactics in this round?
- Round 3:
  - How does establishing a WIP limit help in delivery and reducing [paper] wastage?
  - What else did teams learn or observe in this round?

- **Tips and Tricks:**
  - The Facilitators are encouraged to try variations of this game.

- **Reader Notes:** (Write possible variations and notes below.)
  - ☐ _____
  - ☐ _____
  - ☐ _____

- **Best Time to Play:**

KICK-OFF	PLAN	DO	CHECK	ADJUST
Initiate	*Plan*	*Perform*	*Monitor*	*Improve*

- **Source:** Unknown.

- **Author Notes:** A fun game. As a facilitator, I observed positive competition from all the teams as they made working airplanes. I remember one participant (who was playing the business role) walking up to me and saying, "This is the simplest way of showing how much [paper] wastage is created when the requirements aren't clear." The expression on this person's face was genuine, and the mission was accomplished.

Win-Win Agile Games. Trusted teams for improved results.

CLASSIFY FEATURES

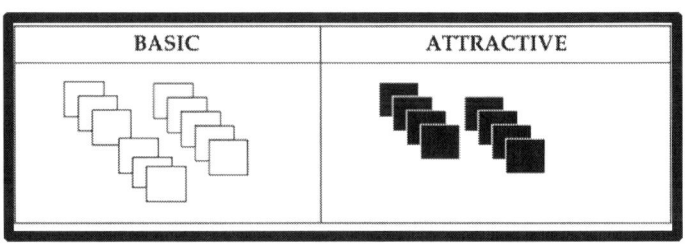

BASIC	ATTRACTIVE

PC: *Classify Features*

- **Game Categories:**

Team Building	Professional Coaching	Retrospectives	Leadership	Others

- **Game Name:** Classify Features
- **Objective:** Play this game to prioritize product features. Basic features are a *must-have* functionality. Attractive features are good to have. Streamline the business team's thoughts and expectations through this game.
- **Facilitator:** A coach, trainer, or Scrum master.
- **Suggested Attendees:** Product owner, subject matter experts (SMEs), and customers.
- **Required Materials:** Conference room, fake currency, flip chart, pens, and sticky notes.
- **Prerequisites:**

- Create a list of business features along with priorities. For example, make a list of features suggested by end-users or implemented by competitors that can be suggested as a part of market analysis.

- **Instructions:**
  - Form groups of four to six people.
  - Two questions are posed to those playing the customers in the game:
    1. Identify a list of features that are "*basic*" or that represent a must-have functionality.
    2. Identify a list of features that are "*attractive*" or improve performance.
  - Customers are asked to categorize features into two buckets: basic and attractive.

- **Timing:**
  - 45–60 minutes, depending upon the number of rounds
    - Exercise: 10–30 minutes
    - Debrief: Remaining time

- **Suggested questions for debriefing:**
  - What are the *basic* features expected by customers?
  - What features can go into *attractive* category?
  - Will any of the attractive features fall under the basic features after discussion?

- ❑ Did attendees add new features? If yes, what has helped them to create new features?
- **Variations:**
  - ❑ Customers are given various choices:
    - ❑ Must have, should have, could have, and wouldn't have (MoSCoW)
    - ❑ Basic, incremental, upgrades, and enhancements
    - ❑ Love it, maybe later, not interested, and no way
- **Tips and Tricks:**
  - ❑ The Facilitator should provide a basic definition of basic versus attractive features before starting the game to attendees.
  - ❑ The Facilitators are encouraged to try variations of this game.
- **Reader Notes:** (Write possible variations and notes below.)
  - ❑ _____
  - ❑ _____
  - ❑ _____
- **Best Time to Play:**

KICK-OFF	PLAN	DO	CHECK	ADJUST
Initiate	*Plan*	*Perform*	*Monitor*	*Improve*

- **Source:** Unknown.
- **Author Notes:** I played this game with team members who were planning a greenfield project. Everyone wanted all the features on

day 1, and the sorting of features was completed in five minutes. As a facilitator, I added an additional rule that stated that each participant could have only two features under the "basic" or "must" category. One feature would be of their choice and another feature would be an acknowledgment from at least one of the other attendees. I observed that this has resulted in increased participation, discussion, and brainstorming among participants to rearrange the features between the basic versus attractive buckets. The revised list is more solid than that of the initial round.

DEFINITION OF OUT AND READY (DOOR)

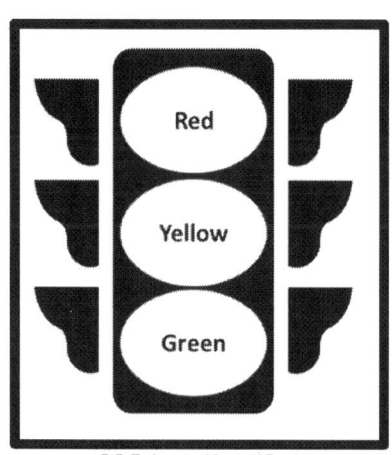

PC: Definition of Out and Ready

- **Game Categories:**

Team Building	Professional Coaching	Retrospectives	Leadership	Others

- **Game Name:** Definition of Out and Ready (DoOR)
- **Objective:** Play this game to help teams understand the importance of user story readiness with high clarity. A clearly defined user story results in fairly accurate estimation, prompt commitment, and timely delivery by Scrum teams. As per Bill Wake's mnemonic INVEST, a user story must be independent, negotiable, valuable, estimable, small, and testable. In short, a user story should contain all the necessary information for teams to understand and commit

to for delivery. It should contain the requirement description and acceptance criteria. This game provides clarity on the importance of a clearly defined user story.

- **Facilitator:** A coach, trainer, or Scrum master.
- **Suggested Attendees:** Product owner, and Scrum team(s).
- **Required Materials:** Conference room, pens, and questions sheet.
- **Prerequisites:** Logistics planning.
- **Instructions:**
  - ❏ Form groups of five to eight people.
  - ❏ Round 1
    - ❏ The Product owner gives instructions to teams verbally and asks the teams to draw a picture.
      - ❏ Keep the instructions vague. For example, instructions to describe a certain animal such as a zebra will be, "It's a four-legged animal with stripes."
    - ❏ Nominate a member from each team to debrief after they are done with the drawing.
    - ❏ The team that meets the Product owner's acceptance criteria gets a scoring point.
    - ❏ There is a possibility that all team members may not interpret the drawing in the same way, resulting in multiple different pictures within a group.

- Round 2
  - The Product owner provides more detailed instructions to teams verbally as well as acceptance criteria.
    - For example:
      - "It's a four-legged animal with black and white stripes."
      - "It's not a pet."
  - Nominate a member from each team to debrief after the drawing.
  - The team that meets the Product owner's acceptance criteria gets a scoring point.
  - The chances of all team members' interpreting the drawing in the same way are much higher due to detailed instructions.

- **Timing:**
  - 30–45 minutes
    - Round 1: 3–5 minutes
    - Debrief on round 1: 5 minutes
    - Round 2: 3–5 minutes
    - Debrief on round 2: Remaining time

- **Suggested questions for debriefing:**
  - Is the user story ready in round 1?
  - What did teams learn from round 1?
  - Did the Product owner accept the deliverable in round 1?

- ❑ What changed in round 2?
- ❑ Did teams contact the Product owner during the exercise to validate the product?
- ❑ How did teams define user story readiness?
- ❑ What did teams learn from the exercise?
- ❑ Are there any additions required to the game?

- **Tips and Tricks:**
  - ❑ The Facilitators are encouraged to try variations of this game.
  - ❑ The Facilitator can encourage the teams to ask the Product owner the right questions to understand the user story so they can deliver the right product. They can also interact with the Product owner as they draw to make sure the picture aligns with the user story requirements.
  - ❑ Consider small prizes for the winning team.

- **Reader Notes:** (Write possible variations and notes below.)
  - ❑ _____
  - ❑ _____
  - ❑ _____

- **Best Time to Play:**

KICK-OFF	PLAN	DO	CHECK	ADJUST
Initiate	*Plan*	*Perform*	*Monitor*	*Improve*

- **Source**: Savitha Katham. If you know any games with similarities, please send the details to our team at phenombooksllc@gmail.com.

- **Author Notes**: While coaching Scrum teams, one frequent question came to my attention: *Was the user story ready for commitment?* Sprint planning durations extended when the Product owner and team members didn't reach a consensus. I played this game to solidify the understanding of user story readiness so that teams could review the business needs, document assumptions, estimate the effort, and then commit.

EMPATHY MAP

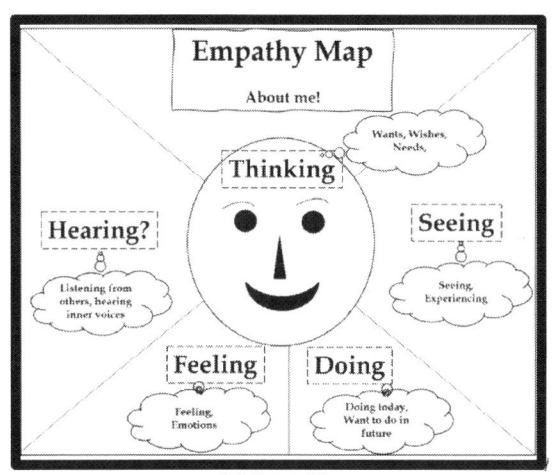

PC: Empathy Map

- **Game Categories:**

| Team Building | Professional Coaching | Retrospectives | Leadership | Others |

- **Game Name:** Empathy Map
- **Objective:** Play this game to understand personas and their choices and preferences while building a product.
- **Facilitator:** A coach, trainer, or Scrum master.
- **Suggested Attendees:** Business leads, business SMEs, sponsors, architects, and application leads.
- **Required Materials:** Conference room, pens, papers, flip charts, and wall adhesives.

- **Prerequisites:**
  - ❏ Before the game starts, ensure the group has a detailed description of the project and a list of the individuals involved in the project (including their names, occupations, ages, and locations).

- **Instructions:**
  - ❏ Form groups of four to six people.
    - ❏ The facilitator provides the project description and asks the attendees to write down what each person/role is (as shown in the picture):
      - ❏ Thinking
      - ❏ Seeing
      - ❏ Hearing
      - ❏ Saying
      - ❏ Feeling
      - ❏ Doing
    - ❏ The group should try to identify and document these aspects in creating their persona:
      - ❏ What does this person want?
      - ❏ What forces are motivating this person?
      - ❏ What can we do for this person?

- **Timing:**
  - ❏ 45–60 minutes

- ❏ Introduction: 5–10 minutes
- ❏ Groups working on personas: 20 minutes
- ❏ Debrief: Remaining time

- **Suggested questions for debriefing:**
  - ❏ Were teams able to identify the end-users?
  - ❏ Did the teams find personas that are close to real-life people while developing the product?
  - ❏ Are the selected personas the right ones for the product?
  - ❏ Was any persona irrelevant to the discussion?
  - ❏ Why was a certain age group chosen as personas?

- **Tips and Tricks:**
  - ❏ The Facilitators are encouraged to try variations of this game.
  - ❏ You can use the Empathy Map for retrospective meetings to understand the reaction of Scrum teams on the completed sprint(s).

- **Reader Notes:** (Write possible variations and notes below.)
  - ❏ _____
  - ❏ _____
  - ❏ _____

- **Best Time to Play:**

KICK-OFF	PLAN	DO	CHECK	ADJUST
Initiate	*Plan*	*Perform*	*Monitor*	*Improve*

- **Source**: David Gray.

- **Author Notes:** I presented this game at an Agile Games conference. The reception from attendees was positive. The questions I wrote on the flip chart were: Does a product need to be based on 1) the investor's choice? or 2) the customer's choice? Before the game, attendees chose "investor" because the investor is putting the money, creativity, and time. During the debrief after the game, everyone agreed the "customer" persona plays a key role in the success of a product. Clarity achieved!

EFFECTIVE TEAMS

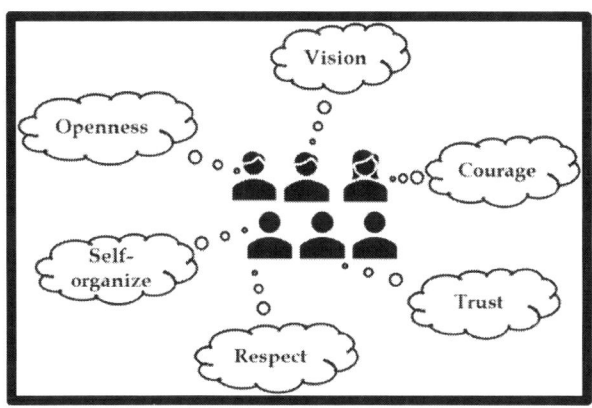

PC: Effective Teams

- **Game Categories:**

Team Building	Professional Coaching	Retrospectives	Leadership	Others

- **Game Name:** Effective Teams
- **Objective:** Play this game to coach teams on how to become highly efficient.
- **Facilitator:** A coach, trainer, or Scrum master.
- **Suggested Attendees:** Product owner, and Scrum team(s).
- **Required Materials:** Conference room, pens, sticky notes, and a prepared list of keywords (written on sticky notes).
- **Prerequisites:** Logistics planning.
- **Instructions:**

- ❑ Form groups of four to six people.
- ❑ Give three sticky notes to each participant and ask them to write three keywords that describe the characteristics or traits of effective teams based on their personal experience or knowledge.
- ❑ Collect all the sticky notes from the participants and add them to the already prepared list of keywords. (See Appendix A at the end of this game for the list of prepared keywords.)
- ❑ Give each participant three sticky notes from the mixed-up stack and ask them to prioritize the keywords in order of importance.
- ❑ Each team consolidates the keywords from every team member and selects the top three keywords for their team. For example, if a team has five members, there will be 15 keywords from which they will need to select the top three.
- ❑ Each team explains why they believe those keywords are essential for a team to be efficient.

- **Timing:**
    - ❑ 30–45 minutes
        - ❑ Individuals writing three keywords: 5–10 minutes
        - ❑ Consolidating all keywords and distributing three keywords to each person: 5–10 minutes
        - ❑ Forming teams and coming up with three keywords for each team: 15 minutes
        - ❑ Debrief: Remaining time

- **Suggested questions for debriefing:**
  - ❑ Did any individual play a big part while prioritizing the characteristics?
  - ❑ What are the most repeated keywords?
  - ❑ Why are those keywords important for the teams?
  - ❑ What characteristics did teams chose that they have right now?
  - ❑ What characteristics are teams planning to acquire for future sprints?
  - ❑ Are there any team members who did not participate in the discussions? If yes, what measures can be taken to increase their participation?

- **Variations:**
  - ❑ Provide three keywords for each team from the prepared list.
  - ❑ Ask them to draw a picture of each keyword.
  - ❑ One team member from each team will come forward and show their picture so that other teams will identify the character definition. (Pictures are the result of each team's creativity. No hints are to be given by the facilitator.)

- **Tips and Tricks:**
  - ❑ Create an open environment for team members to speak up.
  - ❑ Try to focus on team members who speak less or shy away from participation.

- ❏ Group interaction and cross-team communication are important, and the facilitator must watch how teams are interacting and discuss this aspect during the debrief.
- ❏ The Facilitators are encouraged to try variations of this game.

- **Reader Notes:** (Write possible variations and notes below.)
  - ❏ _____
  - ❏ _____
  - ❏ _____

- **Best Time to Play:**

KICK-OFF	PLAN	DO	CHECK	ADJUST
Initiate	*Plan*	*Perform*	*Monitor*	*Improve*

- **Source:** Unknown.
- **Author's Note:** I might have played this game more than 50 times. This game is most exciting to me, as I have seen teams coming up with a list of adjectives. Interestingly, in many games, two keywords are commonly picked up by all teams, although these team members have never met each other. They are 1) trust and 2) respect. I have witnessed that team members with good trust levels, and mutual respect makes for highly efficient teams.

Appendix A: Characteristics of Effective Teams:

1. Common vision
2. Clear goals (project and sprint goals)
3. Plan (for reaching the goal)
4. Clarity (on roles and responsibilities)
5. Focus (on the delivery)
6. Respect (for peer team members)
7. Commitment (to the deliverables and their success)
8. Courage (to take more challenges and speak up for help)
9. Openness (to address challenges and work with team members on the mitigations)
10. Trust (within the team)
11. Decentralization (decision-making)
12. Accountability
13. Self-coordination
14. Shared responsibility
15. Thriving environment
16. Continuous improvement opportunity
17. Self-assessment
18. Shared leadership
19. Small team size
20. Empowerment
21. Effective stakeholder relationships
22. Effective interpersonal skills
23. Generalists
24. Self-organizing
25. Safe environment

FORCED RANKING

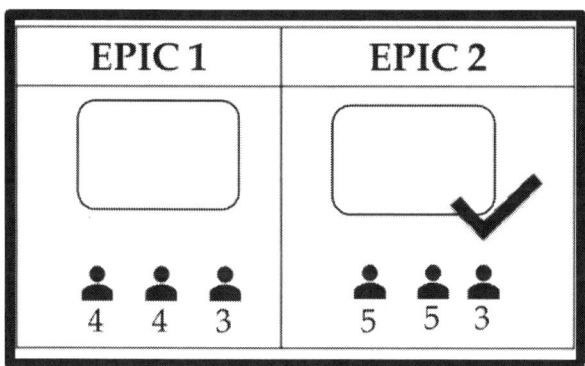

PC: Forced Ranking

- **Game Categories:**

| Team Building | Professional Coaching | Retrospectives | Leadership | Others |

- **Game Name:** Forced Ranking
- **Objective:** Play this game to bring consensus on items that need immediate attention. Ideas with a high number of votes will be prioritized first for implementation. If a particular idea does not get enough votes, then attendees are given an opportunity to discuss and update the assumptions and vote again.
- **Facilitator:** A coach, trainer, or Scrum master.
- **Suggested Attendees:** Product owner, mid-management, and subject matter experts (SMEs).
- **Required Materials:** Conference room, pens, and a flip chart.

- **Prerequisites:**
  - ❑ List of around 10 epics, or ideas, ready for discussion, including:
    - ❑ Business and technical features of a product.
    - ❑ Ideas to evaluate technology for industrial automation.
- **Instructions:**
  - ❑ Form groups of eight to twenty people.
  - ❑ Write each epic and its description on a sticky note and paste it on the wall. Every attendee will read all the epics and descriptions after the consolidation.
  - ❑ Attendees will rank each item based on:
    - ❑ Business value
    - ❑ Technology impact
    - ❑ Cost of delay—i.e., impact on the business if the product is not in the market on time
  - ❑ Attendees are given a scale of 1 to 5, 5 being high impact and 1 being low impact.
  - ❑ All attendees should give their rating after reading each topic based on their experience, knowledge, empirical data, and cognitive traits. They can provide a score between 1 and 5.
  - ❑ After voting, the facilitator counts the votes for each topic received. The results are written on sticky notes and placed near the respective epics. The epic with the highest points will be considered for immediate discussion.

Win-Win Agile Games. Trusted teams for improved results.

Epic	Role	Business Impact	Technology Impact	Cost of Delay	Total	Grand Total	Forced Ranking
Create Online eLearning site	Product Mgr.	4	4	1	9		
	Product Owner	5	4	4	13		
	SME	4	4	4	12		
	Architect	5	4	4	13		
	Tech Lead	4	4	4	12	59	1
Upgrade Windows	Product Manager	2	2	2	6		
	Product Owner	3	3	3	9		
	SME	2	2	2	6		
	Architect	3	3	3	9		
	Tech Lead	2	2	3	7	37	2

PC: *Forced Ranking*

- **Timing:**
    - ❏ 30–45 minutes (depending on the agenda or number of topics)
        - ❏ Introduction: 5–10 minutes
        - ❏ Balance time for discussion
        - ❏ Debrief: 10–15 minutes

- **Suggested questions for debriefing:**
    - ❏ Did teams get a chance to understand all the issues?
    - ❏ How does group rating results differ from individual ratings?
    - ❏ Did teams collaborate before voting?

- **Variations:**
    - ❏ If attendees believe the item that needs immediate attention is not on the top list, they can create new ranking criteria that provide a revised top items list.

- **Tips and Tricks:**
    - ❏ Be open to additional suggestions to play this game creatively.
    - ❏ Interaction between the participants is encouraged.

- **Reader Notes:** (Write possible variations and notes below.)
  - ☐ _____
  - ☐ _____
  - ☐ _____

- **Best Time to Play:**

KICK-OFF	PLAN	DO	CHECK	ADJUST
Initiate	*Plan*	*Perform*	*Monitor*	*Improve*

- **Source:** Unknown.

- **Author Notes:** This game simplified program selection within a department's portfolio for one of my clients. The business's expectations was not aligned with other cross-matrixed department leads in selecting programs for implementation prior to the game. This game was a lifesaver. During the game, all participants discussed assumptions and dependencies and by the end of it, everyone was on the same page on what program(s) should be considered for implementation next. Decision-making was much faster, along with unanimous consensus from all department leads.

KANO MODEL

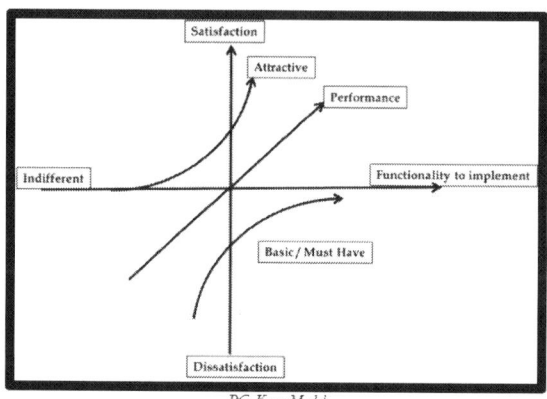

PC: Kano Model

- **Game Categories:**

| Team Building | Professional Coaching | Retrospectives | Leadership | Others |

- **Game Name:** Kano Model
- **Objective:** Play this game to determine customers' satisfaction with product features.
- **Facilitator:** A coach, trainer, or Scrum master.
- **Suggested Attendees:** Product owners, and customers.
- **Required Materials:** Conference room, flip chart, sticky notes of various sizes, and pens.
- **Prerequisites:**

- ❏ Participants must have a better understanding of the product, or product documentation must be shared with participants before this exercise.
- ❏ The Kano model graph should be drawn on a flip chart or a whiteboard (see picture above).
  - ❏ The graph is divided into four quadrants.
  - ❏ *Satisfaction* is the top vertical line.
  - ❏ *Indifferent* is the middle bar, representing that customers are not affected by the presence or absence of features.
  - ❏ The top-right quadrant shows the *attractive* and *performance* features that get the customer's support.
  - ❏ The bottom-right quadrant shows *must-have* features and mandatory features of the product.

- **Instructions:**
  - ❏ Form groups of four to six people.
  - ❏ The business lead or facilitator poses two questions to product management concerning what customers look for in a product:
    - ❏ Identify a list of features that are *basic* or that include must-have functionality.
    - ❏ Identify a list of features that are *attractive* or that improve performance.
  - ❏ Features are later categorized based on the responses on the graph.

- **Timing:**
  - ❑ 45–60 minutes, depending upon the number of sprints played
    - ❑ Exercise: 10–30 minutes
    - ❑ Debrief: Remaining time

- **Suggested questions for debriefing:**
  - ❑ What are the *basic* features expected by customers?
  - ❑ Which are the *attractive* features?
  - ❑ Did any features move from the *attractive* category to the *basic*?
  - ❑ Was there any discussion about multiple product releases due to increased scope?

- **Variations:**
  - ❑ Try variations of categories. Instead of basic and attractive, use MoSCoW (developed by Dai Clegg).
    - ❑ *Must have*: Mandatory features that are included with the base product
    - ❑ *Should have*: Enhanced product features
    - ❑ *Could have*: Good to have at some point, but required right now
    - ❑ *Wouldn't have*: I wouldn't bother to have these features in the product

- **Tips and Tricks:**
  - ❑ Customers may need some direction in understanding basic versus good-to-have features; the facilitator should provide the definitions.

- **Reader Notes:** (Write possible game variations and notes below.)
  - ❑ _____
  - ❑ _____
  - ❑ _____

- **Best Time to Play:**

KICK-OFF	PLAN	DO	CHECK	ADJUST
Initiate	*Plan*	*Perform*	*Monitor*	*Improve*

- **Source:** Noriaki Kano.

- **Author Notes:** This is the best game to play to make the product management teams think. As a facilitator, this game always helped me to bring out the best in new or established product teams by streamlining their energies in identifying prioritized features to be implemented first. I have seen business teams that want all the features as of yesterday. This game helps to stabilize or balance expectations and reality.

Win-Win Agile Games. Trusted teams for improved results.

PRUNE THE PRODUCT TREE

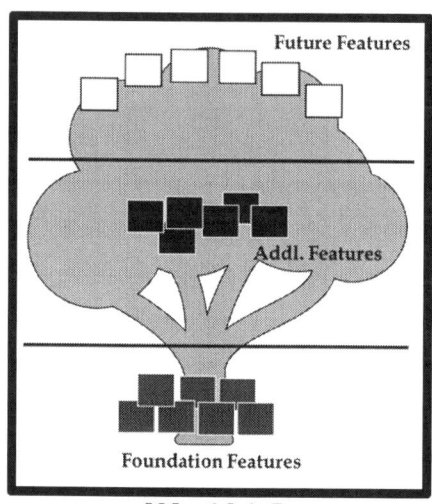

PC: Prune the Product Tree

- **Game Categories:**

Team Building	Professional Coaching	Retrospectives	Leadership	Others

- **Game Name:** Prune the Product Tree
- **Objective:** Play this game to prioritize features with higher business value.
- **Facilitator:** A coach, trainer, or Scrum master.
- **Suggested Attendees:** Product owners, and customers.

- **Required Materials:** Conference room, flip chart, sticky notes of various colors or preprinted leaf-shaped cards and blank leaf-shaped cards, and pens.

- **Prerequisites:**
  - ❑ Draw the tree shape on a flip chart or a whiteboard; making sure the tree is spacious enough so that members can place sticky notes on it.
  - ❑ Write existing features on sticky notes and attach them to the tree to prune. If possible, share an existing features list with the attendees before the exercise.
  - ❑ Write new features that customers want to add to the tree and place them around the tree. Each sticky note should have the name of a feature on the front and the benefit on the back, providing enough detail for the exercise to be successful. The facilitator should remind customers that the shape of the tree represents growth over time.

- **Instructions:**
  - ❑ Form groups of four to six people.
  - ❑ Assign each group to a tree.
  - ❑ Groups should identify the shape and type of tree to represent the product (for example, oak, pine, or apple).
    - ❑ Thick limbs represent major areas of functionality within the system.

- ❑ Leaves near the trunk represent current features.
- ❑ Leaves outside the tree represent new features.
- ❑ The edge of the tree represents the future.
- ❑ Roots of the tree represent reliable infrastructure and a support system.
- ❑ Make sure to display the tree shape on a flip chart or a whiteboard.
  - ❑ The Facilitator requests the customers to place existing features or mandatory features near the trunk.
  - ❑ The leaves closest to the trunk represent features to be added in the near future.
  - ❑ The leaves at tree's edges and beyond represent features to be added in the long term.

- **Timing:**
  - ❑ 45–90 minutes, depending upon the number of sprints played
    - ❑ Exercise: 10–50 minutes
    - ❑ Debrief: Remaining time

- **Suggested questions for debriefing:**
  - ❑ Did the tree become lopsided or too overloaded on one side? Was it crammed with too many features for the near future?
  - ❑ What features were pruned, keeping the tree shape intact?
  - ❑ Did teams discuss and decide on which features to consider for the near term?

- ❑ How did teams decide on what features would be implemented in the near-term and which would be set aside for the long term?
- ❑ What's the release time for the near-term features?
- ❑ What new features were added?
- ❑ How fast do the customers want the tree to grow?
- ❑ Did teams have a difference of opinion on mandatory features? If so, how was the conflict resolved?

- **Variations:**
  - ❑ Customers can put time frames or release schedules on the tree to show growth potential and state the time frame for the near-term and long-term development.

- **Tips and Tricks:**
  - ❑ The Facilitators are encouraged to try variations of this game.
  - ❑ Customers may get too attached to the drawing of a tree. The facilitator must emphasize that the rest of the exercise is to be carried out keeping the tree drawing effort to a minimum.

- **Reader Notes:** (Write possible variations and notes below.)
  - ❑ _____
  - ❑ _____
  - ❑ _____

- **Best Time to Play:**

KICK-OFF	PLAN	DO	CHECK	ADJUST
Initiate	*Plan*	*Perform*	*Monitor*	*Improve*

- **Source:** Luke Hohmann.

- **Author Notes:** The attendees always feel intense while playing this game. It's not easy to categorize features into short-term and long-term needs. This game doesn't result in prioritized features if key business representatives are missing. I remember playing this game on a technology upgrade program to bring technical complexity, dependencies, and assumptions upfront to get support from identified stakeholders. For example, a browser upgrade has resulted in training the Customer Support team on how to access the application in both old and new browser versions. The aha moment for attendees was the importance of their involvement in prioritizing both business and technical product features.

DOT VOTING

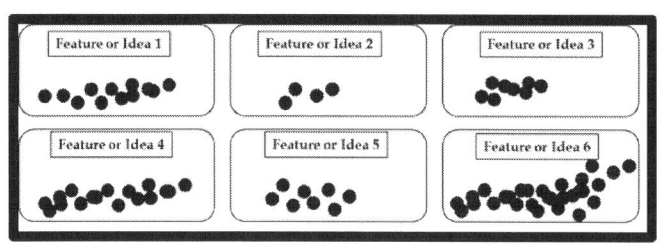

PC: Dot Voting

- **Game Categories:**

Team Building	Professional Coaching	Retrospectives	Leadership	Others

- **Game Name:** Dot Voting
- **Objective:** Play this game to select the best new ideas or to prioritize action items. This game highlights expectations versus reality. Team members reach a unanimous consensus on what issues need to be looked at first. This game is suitable for bringing out creative ideas from innovation hackathons.
- **Facilitator:** A coach, trainer, or Scrum master.
- **Suggested Attendees:** Product owner, Scrum team(s), or customers.
- **Required Materials:** Conference room, pens, and dot voting sheets.
- **Prerequisites:** Logistics planning.
- **Instructions:**

- ❑ Survey participants to collect ideas (or features associated with the specific theme) in advance. For example, ideas on a new product, or enhancements for an existing product.
- ❑ Post the list of collected ideas on a wall using sticky notes.
- ❑ Attendees should read all the topics listed.
- ❑ Attendees vote, in front of the group, for topics by using a pen and putting a dot on the topic or by using dots from the sheets.
- ❑ Each attendee gets five dots (each dot equals one vote). Attendees can use more than one dot to vote an idea. If they feel strongly about one idea, they can use all five dots to vote on a single idea.
- ❑ The topics that get the highest number of votes are prioritized for further discussion.

- **Timing:**
  - ❑ 45–60 minutes, based on the agenda or number of topics to be covered
    - ❑ Reading ideas: 15–25 minutes
    - ❑ Voting: 5–10 minutes
    - ❑ Debrief: Remaining time

- **Suggested questions for debriefing:**
  - ❑ Did this exercise help in getting immediate attention on pressing issues?

- ☐ Was there any team participation and consensus during the exercise?
- ☐ What did teams do in case a critical issue that did not get a high number of votes?

- **Variations:**
  - ☐ Use funny stickers instead of dots.
  - ☐ Define various color codes to highlight the prioritization of topics. For example, use red dots for ideas with high priority and need immediate attention, yellow for medium priority, and so on.
  - ☐ Be open to additional suggestions to play this game creatively.

- **Tips and Tricks:**
  - ☐ The Facilitators are encouraged to try variations of this game.
  - ☐ Be open to additional suggestions to play this game creatively.

- **Reader Notes:** (Write possible variations and notes below.)
  - ☐ _____
  - ☐ _____
  - ☐ _____

- **Best Time to Play:**

KICK-OFF	PLAN	DO	CHECK	ADJUST
Initiate	*Plan*	*Perform*	*Monitor*	*Improve*

- **Source:** Unknown.

- **Author Notes:** I have facilitated this game in innovation workshops to bring new technology ideas to automate business solutions. Attendees liked that every idea received recognition on the wall. One takeaway was, "I'm glad we all agreed to focus on that technology upgrade idea. I am happy with this quick and easy exercise." It proved once again that games are the means to reach ultimate outcomes.

Win-Win Agile Games. Trusted teams for improved results.

OPEN SPACE

PC: Open Space

- **Game Categories:**

| Team Building | Professional Coaching | Retrospectives | Leadership | Others |

- **Game Name:** Open Space
- **Objective:** Play this game to generate thoughts on various topics and get ideas from a diverse audience. It's like an unconference, or a participant-driven meeting, only with a theme (but without a specific agenda prepared in advance.) Attendees create an agenda during the event and either seek answers to their topics of interest

or visit other attendee sessions to learn or provide input. Open Space, a self-organizing event, brings out answers to complex problems. It encourages a collective brain dump to address issues, create solutions, and generate ideas for growth.

- **Facilitator:** A coach, trainer, or Scrum master.
- **Suggested Attendees:** Product owner, subject matter experts (SMEs), Scrum team(s), and customers.
- **Required Materials:** Large conference room with wide walls, pens, sticky notes, and chairs.
- **Prerequisites:**
  - ❏ Logistics planning.
  - ❏ Create posters of Open Space principles, and Law of two feet
- **Instructions:**
  - ❏ Attendees can range from 50–500, as it is an open-invitation event.
  - ❏ Chairs should be arranged in a circular fashion in the open space model, with added layers of circles as needed (See picture above).
  - ❏ The attendance is based on the *Open Space principles*, meaning that whoever is interested in contributing or learning can attend the event.
  - ❏ Open Space terminology and familiarity
    - ❏ Open Space principles:

- ❏ Whoever attends are the right people.
- ❏ When it starts, it is the right time.
- ❏ When it's over, it's over.
- ❏ Whatever happens is the only thing that could happen.
❏ The Law of two feet

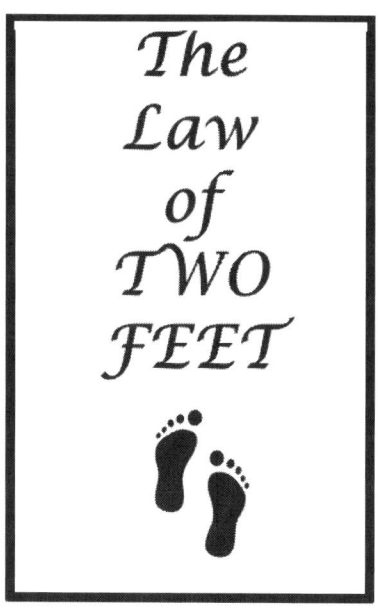

PC: Law of two feet

❏ Open Space attendee roles
  - ❏ **Host**: Speaker of the breakout session.
  - ❏ **Bumblebees**: Attendees who move from one breakout session to another.
  - ❏ **Butterflies**: Attendees who stay in a breakout session in full.
❏ Marketplace

- A place where all issues (topics) are posted on the wall for further discussion.
- The marketplace has a schedule announcing the time and place for sessions.
- Each session can range from 30–45 minutes.

9:30 am	Opening Space (Theme; Process instructions; Market Place)				
10:30 am	15 min Break				
10:45 am	Session 1 (55 min)	Session 2 (55 min)	Session 3 (55 min)	Session 4 (55 min)	Session 5 (55 min)
11:40 am	5 min Transition Time				
11:45 am	Session 6 (55 min)	Session 7 (55 min)	Session 8 (55 min)	Session 9 (55 min)	Session 10 (55 min)
12.40 pm	Lunch				

PC: Market place

- Invite people with different ideas and thought processes. You might want to explore (a) how to increase employee engagement, (b) how to roll out a new product in the East Coast, or (c) how to market a new and improved product.
- Ask attendees to sit in a circle.
- The facilitator announces the theme of the event and asks people to come forward to write issues, ideas, and concerns.
- Attendees write about their topic of interest (contributions), read it out loud to the audience, and post about it on the marketplace.
- Everyone is encouraged to write down their topics.
- The hosts conduct the breakout sessions as noted on the schedule.

- ❑ Other audiences will attend the breakout sessions.
- ❑ All attendees come back to the chairs at the end of all of the sessions, and each attendee gets a chance to reflect on their learnings, discoveries, and next steps.

- **Timing:**
  - ❑ Four hours to one day, depending on the number of attendees

- **Suggested questions for debriefing:**
  - ❑ What did attendees take away from the event?
  - ❑ What did organizers learn from the event?
  - ❑ What are the new challenges that were uncovered?

- **Variations:**
  - ❑ Try with a small group, like a sales group, to experience an Open Space event.

- **Tips and Tricks:**
  - ❑ Identify the best idea or solution from the event and recognize the team or an individual contributor.
  - ❑ The Facilitators are encouraged to try variations of this game.

- **Reader Notes:** (Write possible variations and notes here.)
  - ❑ _____
  - ❑ _____
  - ❑ _____

- **Best Time to Play:**

KICK-OFF	PLAN	DO	CHECK	ADJUST
Initiate	*Plan*	*Perform*	*Monitor*	*Improve*

- **Source:** Harrison Owen.

- **Author Notes:** I learned about Open Space for the first time during Agile Games, New England. All parts of the process—preparation, marketplace, and presentations—were interesting to me. I was a butterfly, meaning that I participated actively in the sessions I liked and learned and shared knowledge and experiences. Fast forward to when I organized an Open Space for a client on an *Agile Transformation and Beyond* topic. The management was very happy to receive valuable feedback. The best part was that the agenda was flexible, and many people flowed in and participated in the idea generation as time permitted. I encourage companies who would like to harvest new ideas enterprise-wide to consider Open Space. The environment is safe and flexible.

Win-Win Agile Games. Trusted teams for improved results.

RETROSPECTIVE GAMES

Win-Win Agile Games. Trusted teams for improved results.

SECRET POT

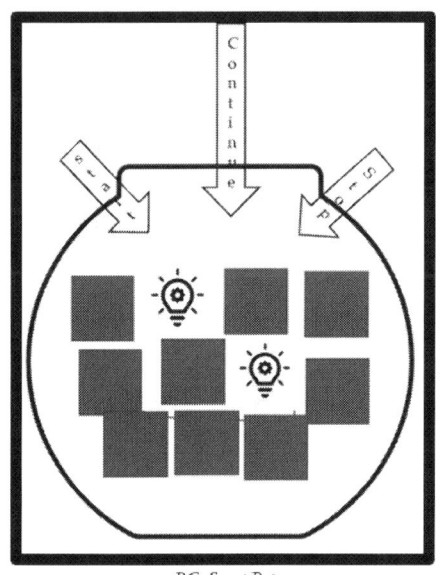

PC: Secret Pot

- **Game Categories:**

| Team Building | Professional Coaching | Retrospectives | Leadership | Others |

- **Game Name:** Secret Pot
- **Objective:** Play this game to learn about the overall performance of a sprint or multiple sprints in-depth, and to collect feedback on leadership and management.
- **Facilitator:** A coach, trainer, or Scrum master.
- **Suggested Attendees:** Product owner and Scrum team(s).

- **Required Materials:** Conference room, sticky notes, and pens.
- **Prerequisites:** Logistics planning.
- **Instructions:**
  - Pose these three questions to the team and ask them to write their answers on sticky notes and put them into the secret pot
    - What should we continue in future sprints? (i.e., what went well)
    - What should we stop in future sprints? (i.e., what didn't go well)
    - What should we start using in future sprints?
  - Keep the Secret Pot in the Scrum room or a place close and accessible to the Scrum team.
  - Collect feedback from the team on an ongoing basis and review the feedback during retrospective sessions at the end of a milestone or a sprint; team members can be anonymous when providing the feedback.
  - Organize a retrospective session; ask the facilitator to read each sticky note aloud. Teams can decide which buckets from the list below the feedback go into.
    - *What to continue?*
    - *What to stop?*
    - *What to start?*
  - Ask the team what they can do to address opportunities for improved performance in future sprints.

- **Timing:**
  - ❑ 15–30 minutes
    - ❑ Exercise: 5–10 minutes
    - ❑ Debrief: Remaining time

- **Suggested questions for debriefing:**
  - ❑ What did teams think of the feedback?
  - ❑ Can teams commit to addressing these action items?
  - ❑ What should teams do differently in future sprints?
  - ❑ Did teams feel safe and secure by providing feedback anonymously?

- **Tips and Tricks:**
  - ❑ Make sure this exercise doesn't end up as a blame game. Encourage each team member in the room to participate in categorizing the feedback. Ask team members who tend to be silent to express their views first.
  - ❑ Having everyone use the same color sticky notes or printed write-ups will encourage team members to express without fear.
  - ❑ The Facilitators are encouraged to try variations of this game.

- **Reader Notes:** (Write possible variations and notes below.)
  - ❑ _____
  - ❑ _____
  - ❑ _____

- **Best Time to Play:**

KICK-OFF	PLAN	DO	CHECK	ADJUST
Initiate	*Plan*	*Perform*	*Monitor*	*Improve*

- **Source:** Unknown.

- **Author Notes:** This game or activity can easily turn into a blame game if instructions are not given appropriately. While playing this game with cross-matrixed teams or at one of the client sites, the outcome can turn into finger-pointing. As a coach, be mindful of your surroundings and take control of the situation quickly to avoid losing the spirit of the game. If required, play an ice-breaker activity, to increase the team's embracement for this game. Highly efficient teams have used this game as a great means to continuously improve. One SME who was showing a *been there done that* attitude mended his ways after honest feedback through this game.

SAILBOAT

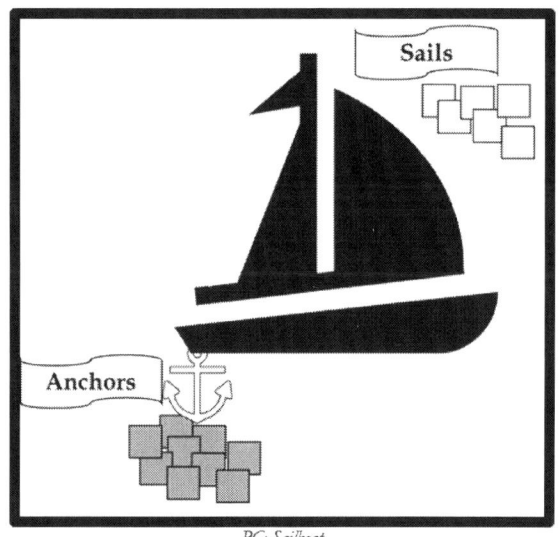

PC: Sailboat

- **Game Categories:**

Team Building	Professional Coaching	Retrospectives	Leadership	Others

- **Game Name:** Sailboat
- **Objective:** Play this game for retrospectives, brainstorming ideas, and for collecting feedback.
- **Facilitator:** A coach, trainer, or Scrum master.
- **Suggested Attendees:** Product owner, subject matter experts (SMEs), Scrum team(s) and stakeholders.

- **Required Materials:** Large conference room with whiteboards and wide, empty walls to paste sticky notes, pens, and chairs.
- **Prerequisites:** Logistics planning.
- **Instructions:**
  - Form groups of seven to nine people.
  - Each group draws a boat on a whiteboard using the above drawing as a guide.
  - A challenge or question is posed to the group.
    - For example: What are the top three issues that caused the last sprint to miss deadlines?
  - Then, each group writes what they liked (worked well) and what they didn't like (challenges, opportunities) during the sprint, on sticky notes and places them under the "sails" and "anchors," respectively. For example, *team collaboration* can be a *sail*.
- **Timing:**
  - 30–45 minutes
    - Exercise: 10–30 minutes
    - Balance time for the debriefing
- **Suggested questions for debriefing:**
  - What are the *anchors* that teams should address before the next sprint?
  - What are the *sails* that the teams appreciate and would like to continue in future sprints?

❑ What did teams learn from this exercise?

- **Tips and Tricks:**
    ❑ The Facilitators are encouraged to try variations of this game.
    ❑ Be ready to hear some harsh feedback from participants.
    ❑ Try grouping similar personalities while organizing this game for a fair balance of voices within each group.
    ❑ This game works well with people who are not comfortable in verbally expressing their emotions. Writing can be a suitable medium for providing feedback. It focuses on what is important and how soon the feedback or input can be implemented.
    ❑ It helps the thinking process by putting all unexpressed or passive-aggressive behaviors in check.

- **Reader Notes:** (Write possible variations and notes below.)
    ❑ _____
    ❑ _____
    ❑ _____

- **Best Time to Play:**

KICK-OFF	PLAN	DO	CHECK	ADJUST
Initiate	*Plan*	*Perform*	*Monitor*	*Improve*

- **Source:** Unknown.

- **Author Notes:** This game is very coach friendly. As a facilitator and a coach, I was successful in bringing out both sails and anchors from the attendees. They could remember all the good things that were helping them to move forward, as well as opportunities that needed immediate attention. Emotions may run high as team members speak about their experiences. As a coach, I have asked *powerful questions* to help them come up with the solutions, prepare the action items, and commit to dates to address them.

Win-Win Agile Games. Trusted teams for improved results.

MEMORY TESTER

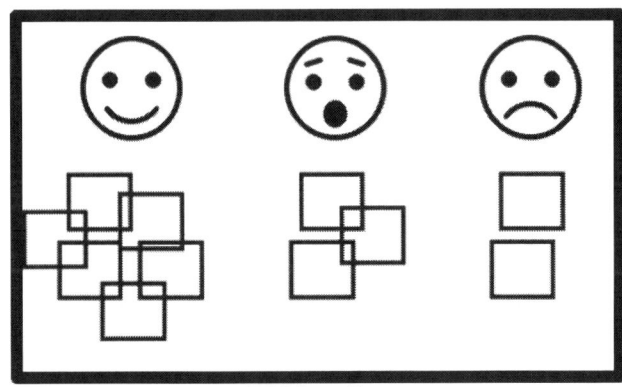

PC: *Memory Tester*

- **Game Categories:**

| Team Building | Professional Coaching | Retrospectives | Leadership | Others |

- **Game Name:** Memory Tester
- **Objective:** Play this game after a sprint, or at a retrospective session, to understand the team's overall satisfaction with a sprint or multiple sprints.
- **Facilitator:** A coach, trainer, or Scrum master.
- **Suggested Attendees:** Product owner and Scrum team(s).
- **Required Materials:** Large conference room with wide walls to paste sticky notes, pens, and a flip chart.
- **Prerequisites:** Logistics planning.

Win-Win Agile Games. Trusted teams for improved results.

- **Instructions:**
  - ❑ Explain the sticky note colors to attendees:
    - ❑ **Red**: Challenging, complex, critical sprint
    - ❑ **Yellow**: Surprising, manageable sprint
    - ❑ **Green**: As planned, on time
  - ❑ Ask the team members to pick the color representing their thoughts and opinions on the sprint(s) and place them on the wall.

- **Suggested questions for debriefing:**
  - ❑ What colors made it to the wall the most?
  - ❑ Why do teams think the sprint(s) represents a specific color?
  - ❑ What experiences have influenced the selection of a specific color?
  - ❑ What can teams do to reduce yellows and reds and increase greens?

- **Tips and Tricks:**
  - ❑ The Facilitators are encouraged to try variations of this game on projects or programs.

- **Reader Notes:** (Write possible variations and notes below.)
  - ❑ _____
  - ❑ _____
  - ❑ _____

- **Best Time to Play:**

KICK-OFF	PLAN	DO	CHECK	ADJUST
Initiate	*Plan*	*Perform*	*Monitor*	*Improve*

- **Source:** Unknown.

- **Author Notes:** As a coach, this game has given me an opportunity to engage teams in continuous improvement. It is a simple and quick game. The aha moments for me are when teams are honest. They come forward genuinely with ideas on improvements that can be implemented to benefit the program and personal goals.

Win-Win Agile Games. Trusted teams for improved results.

PECHAKUCHA

PechaKucha
20 X 20
Images X Seconds

PC: PechaKucha

- **Game Categories:**

Team Building	Professional Coaching	Retrospectives	Leadership	Others

- **Game Name:** PechaKucha
- **Objective:** Play this game to enable team members to share their ideas. You can use this game during retrospectives and ideathons. *Pecha Kucha* (Peh cha-Kuh cha) is the Japanese word for chit chat or lightning talks; the concept *talk less, show more* was created by Astrid Klein and Mark Dytham.
- **Facilitator:** A coach, trainer, or Scrum master.
- **Suggested Attendees:** Product owner, Scrum team(s) and subject matter experts (SMEs).

- **Required Materials:** Conference room, pens, microphone (*optional*) and a flip chart.

- **Prerequisites:**
  - ❏ Costumes if attendees have any.
  - ❏ Presentation decks on the topic.

- **Instructions:**
  - ❏ Form groups of eight to twenty people.
  - ❏ Identify the theme for PechaKucha:
    - ❏ What do teams need to do to increase the delivery rate?
    - ❏ How to reduce tech debt?
    - ❏ How to market a new product?
    - ❏ The topic can be identified on the fly or socialized early on through a flyer. The objective of the game is for participants (individuals or teams) to present a saleable idea to address the theme.
  - ❏ PechaKucha as an individual:
    - ❏ Each attendee has three minutes to talk about his or her saleable idea.
    - ❏ Attendees can use props such as drawings, pictures, presentations, and charts.
    - ❏ If using a slide deck, the rule is 20 X 20: 20 slides with 20 seconds of explanations each.
  - ❏ PechaKucha as a team:

- ❑ All team members brainstorm together.
- ❑ A representative from the team comes forward to talk about the team's saleable idea.
- ❑ Team members can use props like drawings, pictures, presentations, and charts.
- ❑ If using a slide deck, the rule is 20 X 20: (parameters as noted above).

- **Timing:**
  - ❑ 30–45 minutes, depending on the number of attendees
    - ❑ Each person or team has three minutes to present
    - ❑ Debrief: Remaining time

- **Suggested questions for debriefing:**
  - ❑ What did the teams learn from the presented ideas?
  - ❑ What worked well?

- **Variations:**
  - ❑ Presenters wear relevant costumes that match their topic to make it more fun.

- **Tips and Tricks:**
  - ❑ Pecha Kucha is focused on bringing out concise content with less distraction. High energy flows in the room because the presentation time is short and fast-paced.
  - ❑ There may be a high level of engagement from attendees due to the speed of presentations.

❏ Consider combining multiple ideas into one to create an innovation explosion.

- **Reader Notes:** (Write possible variations and notes below.)
  ❏ _____
  ❏ _____
  ❏ _____

- **Best Time to Play:**

KICK-OFF	PLAN	DO	CHECK	ADJUST
Initiate	*Plan*	*Perform*	*Monitor*	*Improve*

- **Source**: Astrid Klein and Mark Dytham.

- **Author Notes:** I learned this game at Agile Games, New England. I was at a speakers' dinner, and one of the organizers asked for our attention. We were told to find a partner and get ready for Pecha Kucha on conference retrospectives. The entire room lit up in no time with laughter as each team came up with witty presentations.

Win-Win Agile Games. Trusted teams for improved results.

COMMUNICATION GAMES

SQUARING THE CIRCLE

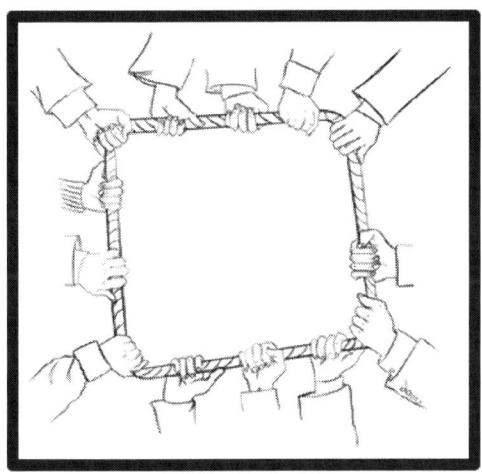

PC: Squaring the circle

- **Game Categories:**

Team Building	Professional Coaching	Retrospectives	Leadership	Others

- **Game Name:** Squaring the Circle
- **Objective:** Play this game as a powerful listening and team-building tool.
- **Facilitator:** A coach, trainer, or Scrum master.
- **Suggested Attendees:** Product owner and Scrum team(s).
- **Required Materials:** Conference room, and a rope.
- **Prerequisites:** Logistics planning.
- **Instructions:**

- Form groups of eight to twenty people.
- Pick a leader to guide teams with instructions.
- Attendee groups stand in two lines facing each other, and a rope is given to one person in the group. The rope is then passed to all attendees to hold. Each attendee should hold the rope with both hands.
- Round 1
  - Team members form a circle while holding the rope with both hands, and then close their eyes.
  - The facilitator provides instructions to the team
  - The leader guides teams to form a shape as per the instructions. He/she has to work with teams to get the expected outcome. For example, the facilitator tells the team to form a square. The leader can guide the teams stating:
    - Michele, go to the right by ten steps.
    - Andrew, go to the left by five steps.
    - Ailey, take two steps to the right.
- Round 2
  - Repeat the instructions and measure the team's improvements.
  - Teams should show improved performance after the round 1 retrospection.

- **Timing:**
  - 30–45 minutes

- ☐ Round 1: 10–15 minutes
- ☐ Debrief Round 1: 5 minutes
- ☐ Round 2: 10–15 minutes
- ☐ Debrief Round 2: Remaining time

- **Suggested questions for debriefing:**
  - ☐ What did the teams learn from this exercise?
  - ☐ Were there feelings of trust among team members in round 1?
  - ☐ What changed in round 2?
  - ☐ What's one thing that teams can take back to their work?
  - ☐ What's one thing you would change to improve the outcome next time?

- **Variations:**
  - ☐ Ask attendees to make a star.

- **Tips and Tricks:**
  - ☐ The Facilitators are encouraged to try additional variations of this game.
  - ☐ Consider small prizes for the winning team.

- **Reader Notes:** (Write possible variations and notes below.)
  - ☐ _____
  - ☐ _____
  - ☐ _____

- **Best Time to Play:**

KICK-OFF	PLAN	DO	CHECK	ADJUST
Initiate	*Plan*	*Perform*	*Monitor*	*Improve*

- **Source**: Booth Sweeney and Dennis Meadows.

- **Author Notes:** This is a good team-building game to learn about business needs at the sprint level through interactions, discussions, and mutual understanding. I have played this game with new scrum teams during their *forming* phase (*Bruck Tuckman's team development stages – forming-storming-norming-performing*) to evaluate their interactions, collaboration and listening skills. This game helped to measure the team's understanding of business needs and sharing the common vision to deliver the expected outcomes. In my experience, the teams that showed good team effort while playing this game evolved into highly efficient teams.

Win-Win Agile Games. Trusted teams for improved results.

BLIND DRAWING

PC: Blind Drawing

- **Game Categories:**

| Team Building | Professional Coaching | Retrospectives | Leadership | Others |

- **Game Name:** Blind Drawing
- **Objective:** Play this game to help teams communicate well with one another, encourage faster decision-making, and to build trust. This game also focuses on how instructions or requirements are interpreted due to miscommunications, and helps to bring out communication challenges.
- **Facilitator:** A coach, trainer, or Scrum master.
- **Suggested Attendees:** Product owner and Scrum team(s).

- **Required Materials:** Conference room, pens, and papers.
- **Prerequisites:** Logistics planning.
- **Instructions:**
  - ❑ Form groups of two to three people.
  - ❑ Give all attendees pens and paper.
  - ❑ Have people sit with their back to the others.
    - ❑ Name each person alphabetically; for example, as A, B, and C.
  - ❑ While drawing, no one looks at the other's picture.
  - ❑ Round 1
    - ❑ Person A draws an image but does not show it to the other team members.
    - ❑ Person A provides instructions to B and C to draw the same picture. The instructions should be directional but not easy and straightforward. For example,
      - ❑ "Draw an apple hanging on a tree," is easy and straightforward.
      - ❑ "Draw a fruit related to Adam and Eve," is directional but not easy and straightforward.
    - ❑ B and C draw their pictures to the best of their ability based on the instructions.
    - ❑ Team members compare their pictures and debrief.
  - ❑ Round 2

- ❏ Repeat the exercise with another illustration by the same set of people. For example, in both rounds, A provides directions and B and C draw the pictures based on the directions.
- ❏ Debrief after the round.

- **Timing:**
  - ❏ 30–45 minutes
    - ❏ Round 1: 10–12 minutes
    - ❏ Round 2: 10–12 minutes
    - ❏ Debrief: Remaining time

- **Suggested questions for debriefing:**
  - ❏ Were instructions clear enough to draw the illustration?
  - ❏ Would use any product-specific features or user stories make it more relatable?
  - ❏ Were team members able to ask questions to clarify the instructions?
  - ❏ What instructions produced better outcomes?
  - ❏ Did you make any progress from round 1 to round 2? If yes, what has helped and what did not?

- **Tips and Tricks:**
  - ❏ The Facilitators are encouraged to try variations of this game.
  - ❏ Be open to additional suggestions to play this game creatively.
  - ❏ Interaction between the participants is encouraged.

❏ Timebox each round.

- **Reader Notes:** (Write possible variations and notes below.)
  ❏ _____
  ❏ _____
  ❏ _____

- **Best Time to Play:**

KICK-OFF	PLAN	DO	CHECK	ADJUST
Initiate	*Plan*	*Perform*	*Monitor*	*Improve*

- **Source:** Unknown.

- **Author Notes:** I presented this game at the Agile Games Conference, New England. I came across it while searching for communication improvement tools between Product owners and Scrum teams. This game reveals potential challenges and assumptions while communicating business requirements from businesses to teams. Built-in trust and respect among the roles help to facilitate constructive conversations, resulting in the effective documentation of needs for predictable delivery. Eight out of ten people did not draw a simple picture correctly in the very first round while playing this game. Teams realized how much effort everyone must put in documenting complex requirements and learned ways to simplify them. My suggestion is to play this game with project team members—of all roles—for increased results.

Win-Win Agile Games. Trusted teams for improved results.

LOST IN TRANSLATION

PC: Lost in Translation

- **Game Categories:**

| Team Building | Professional Coaching | Retrospectives | Leadership | Others |

- **Game Name:** Lost in Translation
- **Objective:** Play this game with distributed teams to increase rapport among roles.
- **Facilitator:** A coach, trainer, or Scrum master.

- **Suggested Attendees:** Product owner, Scrum team(s) (analyst and a developer).
- **Required Materials:** Conference room, pens, papers, and pictures (abstract, animal, or building).
- **Prerequisites:** Logistics planning.
- **Instructions:**
  - Form groups of seven to nine members. Each person has a role: The Product owner provides requirements, the analyst documents the requirements, the developer implements or codes the requirements, and the Scrum master facilitates the game.
  - Round 1
    - The Product owner has a random picture in his or her hand, which he or she describes to the analyst without revealing the picture.
    - The analyst documents the instructions (requirements) on a sticky note and hands them over to the developer.
    - The developer draws the picture based on the instructions.
    - The analyst can ask as many questions as he or she likes to clarify the Product owner's requirements; however, the developer is not allowed to interact with the Product owner.
  - Round 2

- ❏ The Product owner has a random picture in his or her hand and describes the picture to the analyst and the developer at the same time.
- ❏ Both the analyst and the developer can ask as many questions as they like, but the Product owner never shows the picture.
- ❏ The analyst documents the instructions (requirements) on a sticky note and hands them over to the developer.
- ❏ The developer draws the picture as a proof of concept and shows the picture to Product owner before the final product is delivered.
- ❏ Both the analyst and the developer can interact with the Product owner as needed.

- **Timing:**
  - ❏ 45–60 minutes
    - ❏ Round 1: 5–10 minutes
    - ❏ Round 2: 5–10 minutes
    - ❏ Debrief: Remaining time

- **Suggested questions for debriefing:**
  - ❏ Was the outcome in line with the Product owner's requirements?
  - ❏ What went well in rounds 1 and 2?
  - ❏ What did teams learn from each round?

- What would you (teams) do differently next time?

- **Tips and Tricks:**
  - The Facilitators are encouraged to try variations of this game.
  - Use online tools to play this game over a distance.
  - Discuss the challenges and mitigations to understand product needs and implement them.

- **Reader Notes:** (Write possible variations and notes below.)
  - _____
  - _____
  - _____

- **Best Time to Play:**

KICK-OFF	PLAN	DO	CHECK	ADJUST
Initiate	*Plan*	*Perform*	*Monitor*	*Improve*

- **Source:** DocOnDev.

- **Author Notes:** This is a cool game that can be used to help understand a team's rapport. In my experience, team members with great rapport and high levels of mutual understanding get good results. In one instance, a game took more than five sprints to get the expected outcomes (say, documenting and drawing a picture as per business expectations) because there was no trust among the team members. That had a major impact on the overall result.

Win-Win Agile Games. Trusted teams for improved results.

ROPE NOPE

PC: Rope Nope

- **Game Categories:**

Team Building	Professional Coaching	Retrospectives	Leadership	Others

- **Game Name:** Rope Nope
- **Objective:** Play this game to emphasize nonverbal communication skills and collaboration at the management level. This game focuses on listening skills.
- **Facilitator:** A coach, trainer, or Scrum master.
- **Suggested Attendees:** Senior management, mid-management, or Scrum team(s).

- **Required Materials:** Conference room, pens, sticky notes, and ropes (5" in length).
- **Prerequisites:** Logistics planning.
- **Instructions:**
  - ❑ Form groups of four to six people.
  - ❑ Each team gets one long rope.
  - ❑ Tie the two ends of the rope together, forming a circle.
  - ❑ Team members should communicate *nonverbally* throughout this exercise.
  - ❑ Round 1
    - ❑ The facilitator gives each team a sticky note with a shape to make. For example, the sticky note may have "make a circle" as an instruction. Start with a simple shape.
    - ❑ One of the team members can demonstrate or convey the same shape to all team members through hand gestures.
    - ❑ Every team member *must* hold the rope after making the design.
    - ❑ There is a penalty if a team member lets go of the rope or if a team member speaks while providing the instructions.
  - ❑ Round 2
    - ❑ The facilitator gives another sticky note to the team with new shape information.
    - ❑ One of the team members demonstrates or conveys the shape to all team members through hand gestures.

- ❑ Every team member must hold the rope after making the design.
- ❑ There is a penalty if a team member lets go of the rope or if a team member speaks while providing the instructions.

- **Timing:**
  - ❑ 15–30 minutes
    - ❑ Round 1: 10 minutes
    - ❑ Round 2: 10 minutes
    - ❑ Debrief: Remaining time

- **Suggested questions for debriefing:**
  - ❑ How did teams accomplish the task?
  - ❑ What was most helpful in accomplishing the task?
  - ❑ Were there any challenges while communicating nonverbally?
  - ❑ How was round 1 different from round 2? Did teams see any improvements? If yes, what are they?
  - ❑ Does this exercise remind you, (team), of any experiences you've had before?

- **Tips and Tricks:**
  - ❑ The Facilitators are encouraged to try variations of this game.

- **Reader Notes:** (Write possible variations and notes below.)
  - ❑ _____
  - ❑ _____
  - ❑ _____

- **Best Time to Play:**

KICK-OFF	PLAN	DO	CHECK	ADJUST
Initiate	*Plan*	*Perform*	*Monitor*	*Improve*

- **Source**: Savitha Katham.

- **Author Notes:** I remember facilitating this game with a new Scrum team. Teams received this game well, as they quickly moved from being strangers to acquaintances and team players. There was a visible increase in the rapport and bonding amongst the team members during and after the game.

I, YOU, WE

PC: I, You, We

- **Game Categories:**

Team Building	Professional Coaching	Retrospectives	Leadership	Others

- **Game Name:** I, You, We
- **Objective:** Play this game to bring out effective communication in a cross-matrixed environment with high dependencies among departments.
- **Facilitator:** A coach, trainer, or Scrum master.
- **Suggested Attendees:** Senior management, mid-management, or Scrum team(s).

- **Required Materials:** Large conference room, sticky notes, pens, and solitaire playing cards (each team gets a set).
- **Prerequisites:** Logistics planning.
- **Instructions:**
  - ❑ Form groups of four to six people; if the group playing is small, you can play this game with individuals.
  - ❑ The objective is for teams to order the cards by rank.
  - ❑ Round 1
    - ❑ Each group gets two packs of shuffled playing cards (52 cards) distributed among all team members of the team.
    - ❑ Each team must sort shuffled playing cards into a standard deck. The order of sequence should be A, 2, 3, 4, 5, 6, 7, 8, 9, 10, J, Q, K.
    - ❑ The team that completes the sequence first is the winner.
    - ❑ Timebox the event.
  - ❑ Round 2
    - ❑ The facilitator mixes up multiple sets (four packs of cards) of playing cards. For example, if two teams are playing, then four packs of cards are mixed, shuffled, and distributed to each team.
    - ❑ Each team must sort shuffled playing cards into a standard deck. The order of sequence should be A, 2, 3, 4, 5, 6, 7, 8, 9, 10, J, Q, K.

- ☐ No team has the entire stack on a single table, so they have to go to other teams to find—or ask for—the missing cards to complete the sequence.
- ☐ The team that completes the standard deck sequence first is the winner.

- **Timing:**
  - ☐ 30–45 minutes
    - ☐ Round 1: 10–15 minutes
    - ☐ Round 2: 10–15 minutes
    - ☐ Debrief: Remaining time

- **Suggested questions for debriefing:**
  - ☐ What worked well in round 1?
  - ☐ How did teams feel about their mutual dependency in round 2?
  - ☐ What kind of communication tool did teams use to collaborate?
  - ☐ Were any teams slow? If so, did this cause any frustration?
  - ☐ Were there any creative ideas for a win-win situation?
  - ☐ What was the losing team's experience?
  - ☐ How was communication among teams when asking for missing cards?

- **Variations:**
  - ☐ Ask for a sequence of five cards instead of 52 cards.

- **Tips and Tricks:**
  - ☐ The Facilitators are encouraged to try variations of this game.

- **Reader Notes:** (Write possible variations and notes below.)
  - ☐ _____
  - ☐ _____
  - ☐ _____

- **Best Time to Play:**

KICK-OFF	PLAN	DO	CHECK	ADJUST
Initiate	*Plan*	*Perform*	*Monitor*	*Improve*

- **Source:** Savitha Katham.

- **Author Notes:** I customized this game while working on complex programs with high dependencies between a large number of Scrum teams. While playing this game, teams with no dependencies have played well. This game brings clarity on individual team performance versus collaborative teams' performance by acknowledging the dependencies and committing to the delivery of a common vision. Certain teams were uncomfortable when dependencies were identified as they felt it would slow down their individual performances. This game has helped to coach teams and get them on the same page through collaboration.

Win-Win Agile Games. Trusted teams for improved results.

AGILE BINGO

PC: Agile Bingo

- Game Categories:

Team Building	Professional Coaching	Retrospectives	Leadership	Others

- **Game Name:** Agile Bingo
- **Objective:** Play this game for team building and bonding.
- **Facilitator:** A coach, trainer, or Scrum master.
- **Suggested Attendees:** Product owner and Scrum team(s).
- **Required Materials:** Conference room, pens, bingo sheet, and *Scrum guide*[1].
- **Prerequisites:** Logistics planning.
- **Instructions:**

- Form groups of four to six people.
- Give a *Scrum guide* to each group.
- Each team must create a question from the *Scrum guide* and pose it to the next team.
  - For example, Team A creates a question for Team B, and Team B creates a question for Team C. If any team cannot answer a question, it will be passed to the next team.
- Teams are encouraged to frame questions beyond the *Scrum guide* while focusing on Agile to make the activity complex and interesting. See Appendix B below.
  - Examples:
  - Define iterative and incremental software development methodology?
  - Name one core value of Scrum?
  - Name a principle from the Agile Manifesto?

- **Timing:**
  - 30–45 minutes
    - Questions: 15–30 minutes
    - Debrief: Remaining time

- **Suggested questions for debriefing:**
  - What did teams learn from this exercise?
  - Did any teams try to simplify or complicate questions for other teams?

- ❏ Did any team try helping other teams?
- ❏ Did any team ask for help?
- ❏ What worked well for the winning team?

- **Variations:**
  - ❏ Focus on individual and group participation and learning capabilities.

- **Tips and Tricks:**
  - ❏ The Facilitators are encouraged to try variations of this game.
  - ❏ Consider small prizes for the winning team.

- **Reader Notes:** (Write possible variations and notes below.)
  - ❏ _____
  - ❏ _____
  - ❏ _____

- **Best Time to Play:**

KICK-OFF	PLAN	DO	CHECK	ADJUST
Initiate	*Plan*	*Perform*	*Monitor*	*Improve*

- **Source:** Unknown, customized by Savitha Katham.

- **Author Notes:** I played this game after the Scrum training. It is unrealistic to think a two-day training is enough for participants to grasp the foundations of Agile framework and put them into implementation in the workplace. This game helped attendees to read more about Agile, Scrum, and the related framework, keeping the Agile spirit alive. Teams gave unanimous five fingers – *fist of five voting* - for this fun game.

Appendix B: Teams can pick keywords from the bingo card to create questions.

Stand-up	Scrum	Kanban	Sprint
Planning	Agile	Scrum Team	Core Values
Manifesto	Product Owner	Backlog	Refinement
Retrospectives	Estimation	Burndown	Metrics
Paired Programming	Demo	Acceptance Criteria	User Story
Acceptance Criteria	Iteration	Incremental	Scrum Master
devOps	Architecture Runway	TDD	Automation Testing
In-built Quality	Peer Review	Agile Principles	Agile Benefits

Win-Win Agile Games. Trusted teams for improved results.

I AND I (INCREMENTAL AND ITERATIVE)

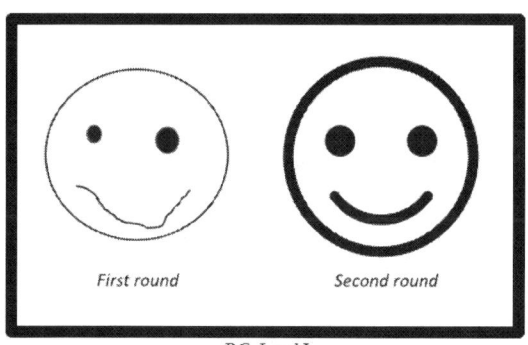

PC: I and I

- **Game Categories:**

| Team Building | Professional Coaching | Retrospectives | Leadership | Others |

- **Game Name:** I and I (Incremental and Iterative)
- **Objective:** Play this game to help teams understand incremental and iterative concepts.
- **Facilitator:** A coach, trainer, or Scrum master.
- **Suggested Attendees:** Scrum team(s).
- **Required Materials:** Conference room, sticky notes, pens, and a whiteboard.
- **Prerequisites:**

- ❑ Create instructions on sticky notes about how to draw a human face. For example, each sticky note should have instructions like: Draw a left eye, draw a right eye, draw eyebrows, draw a nose, draw lips, draw freckles, draw a mole above the lips, and so on.

- **Instructions:**
  - ❑ Form groups of five to eight people.
  - ❑ Teams self-organize into roles such as developers (artists) and testers.
  - ❑ Round 1
    - ❑ Draw a big circle on the whiteboard and give each team one sticky note describing the part of the face they need to draw.
    - ❑ Teams do not show their requirements to each other.
    - ❑ Each team should design the illustration as per the requirements, and validate it with their team first before drawing the feature on the big circle.
    - ❑ All teams should come to the circle and place the drawn parts on the face.
    - ❑ The objective is that the smiley face should be perfect, even though the body parts are drawn by different teams. For example, the size of two eyes drawn by two different teams should be of the same size.
    - ❑ Debrief on the responses.
  - ❑ Round 2
    - ❑ Repeat the same exercise.

- In this round you may see different results, as the teams have had a chance to practice. Expect teams to perform better.
- Debrief on the responses.

- **Timing:**
  - 45–60 minutes
    - Round 1: 10–15 minutes
    - Debrief on round 1: 10 minutes
    - Round 2: 10–15 minutes
    - Debrief: Remaining time

- **Suggested questions for debriefing:**
  - Define incremental and iterative concepts.
  - What did teams learn from round 1 in round 2?
  - How did teams figure out how to match the shape and size of the face parts to make a perfect smiley face?
  - What did teams learn from this exercise?

- **Variations:**
  - Teams can try to play the game with different facial expressions, such as sad or angry.

- **Tips and Tricks:**
  - The Facilitators are encouraged to try additional variations of this game.
  - Consider small prizes for the winning team (i.e., the team whose face looks best).

❏ Timebox each round.

- **Reader Notes:** (Write possible variations and notes below.)
  ❏ _____
  ❏ _____
  ❏ _____

- **Best Time to Play:**

KICK-OFF	PLAN	DO	CHECK	ADJUST
Initiate	*Plan*	*Perform*	*Monitor*	*Improve*

- **Source:** Unknown, customized by Savitha Katham.

- **Author Notes:** As a coach, the easiest way to help attendees learn basic concepts is through participation. This game is very flexible and can be played in multiple variations. I facilitated this game with a product management team for a workshop on backlog creation (*scope decomposition into logical features and user stories to add to the backlog*). The team was very appreciative of the game and its outcomes. One fun fact is that the smiley face was never drawn well by teams on the first attempt. They took more than one round to get to the perfect smiley face.

Win-Win Agile Games. Trusted teams for improved results.

INNOVATE

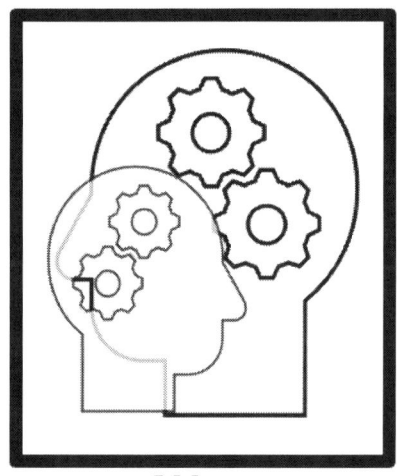

PC: *Innovate*

- **Game Categories:**

Team Building	Professional Coaching	Retrospectives	Leadership	Others

- **Game Name:** Innovate
- **Objective:** Play this game to bring out problem-solving traits in teams focusing on a specific problem.
- **Facilitator:** A coach, trainer, or Scrum master.
- **Suggested Attendees:** Senior management, and mid-management or Scrum team(s).
- **Required Materials:** Conference room, pens, and sticky notes.
- **Prerequisites:** Logistics planning.

- **Instructions:**
  - ❑ Form groups of four to six people; if the group is small, you can play this game as individuals.
  - ❑ Each team creates a story based on the information given by the opposite team. The goal for teams is to match the story as closely as possible based on the instructions.
  - ❑ Round 1: <u>Limited Information</u>
    - ❑ Group A gives a keyword to Group B.
    - ❑ Group B creates a story based on that keyword. For example, Group A's keyword is "trust," and Group B guesses and creates a story around that word.
    - ❑ If the answer is close to Group A's expectations, then Team B wins a point.
    - ❑ It's on Team A to approve the story.
    - ❑ Teams have fun making stories out of keywords.
    - ❑ Debrief on the responses.
  - ❑ Round 2: Detailed Information
    - ❑ In this round, Group A gives a keyword, with additional details, to Group B.
    - ❑ Group B creates a story based on that keyword. For example, Group A's keywords are "trust" and "delivery". Group B guesses and creates a story around those words.

- ❏ Group B is allowed to ask Group A as many questions as they want, but the facilitator should not provide this instruction up-front.
- ❏ If the answer is close to Group A's expectations, then Team B wins a point.
- ❏ It's on Team A to approve the story.
- ❏ Teams have fun making stories out of keywords.
- ❏ Debrief on the responses.

- **Timing:**
  - ❏ 15–30 minutes
    - ❏ Round 1: 10 minutes
    - ❏ Round 2: 10 minutes
    - ❏ Debrief: Remaining time

- **Suggested questions for debriefing:**
  - ❏ How close were you (team) in matching the story as per Group A's expectations in round 1?
  - ❏ What efforts did teams make as they moved to other rounds to better understand the requirements?
  - ❏ What innovative ways have teams provided their requirements to help other teams to create stories?
  - ❏ What was helpful in the game?
  - ❏ Did this game remind you (team) of any experiences from the workplace?

- **Tips and Tricks:**
  ❏ The Facilitators are encouraged to try variations of this game.

- **Reader Notes:** (Write possible variations and notes below.)
  ❏ _____
  ❏ _____
  ❏ _____

- **Best Time to Play:**

KICK-OFF	PLAN	DO	CHECK	ADJUST
Initiate	*Plan*	*Perform*	*Monitor*	*Improve*

- **Source:** Savitha Katham.

- **Author Notes:** : I created this game to facilitate innovation workshops toward building creative solutions around a small idea or unmet demand. For one client, I used this game for technical innovation. The challenge was arriving at "*payment transaction completion in less than two minutes on a mobile application*". The collaboration resulted in uncovering multiple solutions to address this problem. I have used a simplified version of this game during retrospectives ceremonies to bring out opportunities that need to be addressed immediately.

Win-Win Agile Games. Trusted teams for improved results.

CONFLICT GONE

PC: Conflict Gone

- **Game Categories:**

| Team Building | Professional Coaching | Retrospectives | Leadership | Others |

- **Game Name:** Conflict Gone
- **Objective:** This game is played to resolve a conflict between the team members.
- **Facilitator:** A coach, trainer, or Scrum master.
- **Suggested Attendees:** Product owner and Scrum team(s).
- **Required Materials:** Pictures of nature, and a timer.
- **Prerequisites:** Logistics planning.
- **Instructions:**

- Gather the people involved in the conflict. This may be individuals in a one-on-one session, or it might be a group consisting of multiple teams.
- Round 1
  - Timebox: 1 minute per person in an individual setting.
  - The facilitator shows a picture of the sunset to the attendees and asks each team member what comes to their mind when they see that picture.
  - Focus on interpretation and body language.
  - Debrief on the responses.
  - The objective is to understand the conflict's complexity between the people involved and come up with a plan of action to resolve it.
- Round 2
  - Timebox: 1 minute per person in an individual setting.
  - Continue with round 2 as people get warmed up from round 1.
  - The facilitator shows two associated new pictures—for example, of the sunset and birds, to the attendees and asks them what comes to their mind when they see those pictures.
  - Focus on interpretation and body language.
  - Debrief on the responses.

- ❏ The objective is to understand the conflict's complexity between the people involved and come up with a plan of action to resolve it.

- **Suggested questions for debriefing:**
  - ❏ Why do you think person 1's interpretation is different from yours?
  - ❏ What aspects of person 1's perspective interested you?
  - ❏ Did team members interpret the pictures with similar answers, or differently?
  - ❏ Did the facilitator observe any change in body language as members speak up?
  - ❏ Were there any triggers that helped to identify the conflict between the team members or teams? How did you handle them?
  - ❏ If a conflict occurs between teams while creating deliverables at the workplace, how would you address the situation?

- **Tips and Tricks:**
  - ❏ The Facilitators are encouraged to try variations of this game.
  - ❏ Add a third round (#3) and another person to increase the number of perspectives.

Win-Win Agile Games. Trusted teams for improved results.

- **Reader Notes:** (Write possible variations and notes below.)
  - ❏ _____
  - ❏ _____
  - ❏ _____

- **Best Time to Play:**

KICK-OFF	PLAN	DO	CHECK	ADJUST
Initiate	*Plan*	*Perform*	*Monitor*	*Improve*

- **Source:** Unknown, customized by Savitha Katham.

- **Author Notes:** This game is a good coaching tool to measure the intensity of a conflict between team members or between teams. I came across this game during a behavioral training session. Depending on the behavioral responses from the attendees, additional coaching is suggested. Measurable deliverables are suggested where trust, respect, and delivery traits are evaluated with continuous monitoring. It is a simple game that can be a great start in resolving conflicts.

Win-Win Agile Games. Trusted teams for improved results.

ICEBREAKER GAMES

Win-Win Agile Games. Trusted teams for improved results.

HUMAN KNOT

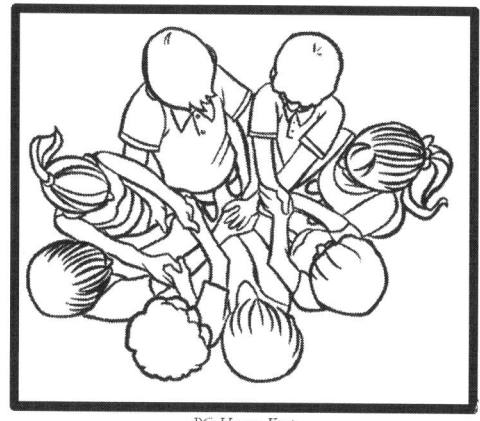

PC: Human Knot

- **Game Categories:**

| Team Building | Professional Coaching | Retrospectives | Leadership | Others |

- **Game Name:** Human Knot
- **Objective:** Play this game for team building.
- **Facilitator:** A coach, trainer, or Scrum master.
- **Suggested Attendees:** Product owner and Scrum team(s).
- **Required Materials:** Conference room, and a flip chart.
- **Prerequisites:** Logistics planning.
- **Instructions:**
  - ❏ Form groups of eight to twenty people.

- [ ] Each team forms a large circle facing in. Everyone should move close enough together so they can reach out and touch the hands of the person opposite them.
- [ ] Each person should then hold hands with two different people in the circle, making sure not to hold the hand of a person directly next to them.
- [ ] After all hands are being held, the group must now try to untangle the knot without releasing their hands.
- [ ] The aim is for the group to work together to untangle themselves so that they can return to a circle of people with clasping hands intact.
- [ ] If more than one team is playing, then teams can compete on the fastest time.

- **Timing:**
  - [ ] 15–30 minutes
    - [ ] Exercise: 5–15 minutes
    - [ ] Debrief: Remaining time

- **Suggested questions for debriefing:**
  - [ ] What did the team learn from this activity?
  - [ ] Did any team players give up in the beginning?
  - [ ] What did it take to get everybody to agree to continue the untangling?
  - [ ] Did team members know one another before the exercise?

- ❏ How easy was it to talk to strangers to achieve a common goal?
- ❏ What was the top challenge while untangling?

- **Variations:**
  - ❏ Bring in rope pieces of approximately one foot in length. There should be the same number of ropes as attendees.
  - ❏ Ask the players to form a circle. Each player should hold one end of the rope, and the other end should be held by someone else in the circle who is not the immediate neighbor.
  - ❏ For example, each attendee has two rope pieces, one in each hand. The other ends of the ropes are held by two different attendees.
  - ❏ Ask the team to untangle back to a circle without losing grip of the ropes. Teams get negative points every time they drop one end of the rope.

- **Tips and Tricks:**
  - ❏ The Facilitators are encouraged to try other variations of this game.
  - ❏ This game requires some physical activity. If some team members cannot hold hands while twisting themselves, then loosen up the rules and allow them to break the clasp.

Win-Win Agile Games. Trusted teams for improved results.

- **Reader Notes:** (Write possible variations and notes below.)
  - ❑ _____
  - ❑ _____
  - ❑ _____

- **Best Time to Play:**

KICK-OFF	PLAN	DO	CHECK	ADJUST
Initiate	*Plan*	*Perform*	*Monitor*	*Improve*

- **Source:** Unknown.

- **Author Notes:** I wish I knew the original author of this game. I would personally shake his or her hand. This is a simple high-energy game where all attendees interact. Even strangers become friends by the end of this game. I can vouch that your teams will enjoy this game thoroughly.

Win-Win Agile Games. Trusted teams for improved results.

KNOW THEM

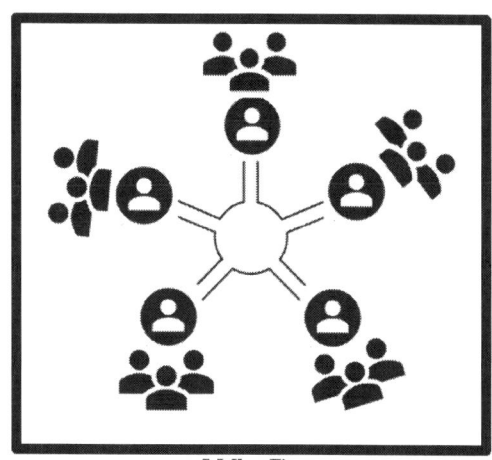

PC: Know Them

- **Game Categories:**

| Team Building | Professional Coaching | Retrospectives | Leadership | Others |

- **Game Name:** Know Them

- **Objective:** Play this game as an ice-breaking activity to learn about new team members during the forming phase.

- **Facilitator:** A coach, trainer, or Scrum master.

- **Suggested Attendees:** Scrum team(s).

- **Required Materials:** Conference room, sticky notes, and pens.

- **Prerequisites:** Logistics planning.

- **Instructions:**
  - ❑ Ask attendees to write down the first word that comes to their mind when they hear the following words: "color" and "flower."
  - ❑ Ask attendees to form a group based on their *color* or *flower* selection; For example, all team members who like the *Blue* color come together and form a group.
  - ❑ The objective is that teams get to learn commonality that bonds them together.

- **Timing:**
  - ❑ 15–30 minutes
    - ❑ Game: 10 minutes
    - ❑ Debrief: Remaining time

- **Suggested questions for debriefing:**
  - ❑ Did teams identify common interests?
  - ❑ What did teams take away from this exercise?

- **Tips and Tricks:**
  - ❑ The Facilitators are encouraged to try variations of this game.

- **Reader Notes:** (Write possible variations and notes below.)
  - ❑ _____
  - ❑ _____
  - ❑ _____

Win-Win Agile Games. Trusted teams for improved results.

- **Best Time to Play:**

KICK-OFF	PLAN	DO	CHECK	ADJUST
Initiate	*Plan*	*Perform*	*Monitor*	*Improve*

- **Source**: Booth Sweeney and Dennis Meadows.

- **Author Notes:** When I think of this game, one thing that comes to my mind is connections. This game instantly connects people through fun words. I have observed team members loosening up during this game to learn more about other team members' interests, which has helped them bond well later.

ESVP

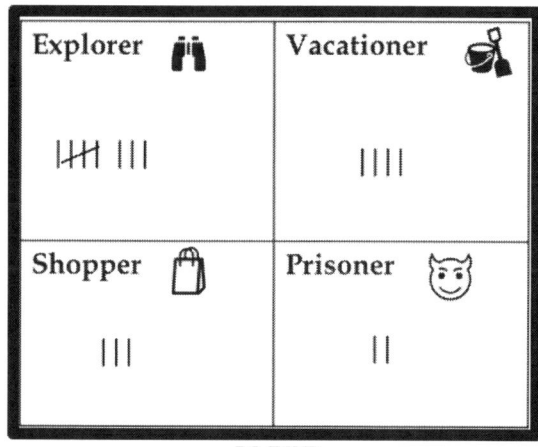

Explorer 👀 ┃┼┼┼ ┃┃┃	Vacationer 🏖️ ┃┃┃┃
Shopper 🛍️ ┃┃┃	Prisoner 😈 ┃┃

PC: ESVP

- **Game Categories:**

Team Building	Professional Coaching	Retrospectives	Leadership	Others

- **Game Name:** ESVP
- **Objective:** Play this game to understand attendees' engagement, mood, or attitude toward meetings.
- **Facilitator:** A coach, trainer, or Scrum master.
- **Suggested Attendees:** Product owner, and Scrum team(s).
- **Required Materials:** Conference room, sticky notes, flip chart, and pens.
- **Prerequisites:** Logistics planning.

- **Instructions:**
  - ❑ Explain ESVP to attendees:
    - ❑ **Explorers**: Quick learners with innovative minds and high grasping power. They look for more ideas to develop.
    - ❑ **Shoppers**: They shop around for info and content with at least one idea.
    - ❑ **Vacationers**: Not interested in the meeting and wish they were not working.
    - ❑ **Prisoners**: Not interested in the meeting and wish they were doing other "productive" work.
  - ❑ Before a meeting begins, provide all attendees with a sticky note and ask them to write down their views on attending the meeting. For example, one of the attendees may write "Explorer" or "E" on his or her sticky note and hands it over to the facilitator.
  - ❑ Attendees are not allowed to show their responses to others.
  - ❑ The facilitator collects the results and draws a histogram of responses.
  - ❑ All responses are kept anonymous.
- **Suggested questions for debriefing:**
  - ❑ How was the team's response?
  - ❑ In which quadrant do you see a spike—*explorers, shoppers, vacationers, or prisoners*?

- ❏ Why did teams choose the prisoner's quadrant? What measures can you take to increase the team's participation or improve the mood?
- ❏ Are the moods mentioned by teams specific only to a single meeting, or are they experiencing these moods throughout the overall project?
- ❏ Did you make any changes to the meeting based on the responses?

- **Tips and Tricks:**
  - ❏ The Facilitators are encouraged to try variations of this game.

- **Reader Notes:** (Write possible variations and notes below.)
  - ❏ _____
  - ❏ _____
  - ❏ _____

- **Best Time to Play:**

KICK-OFF	PLAN	DO	CHECK	ADJUST
Initiate	*Plan*	*Perform*	*Monitor*	*Improve*

- **Source:** Unknown.

- **Author Notes:** This game is a quick warm-up exercise to prepare attendees for a workshop or key meetings. This game helps attendees evaluate how involved they will be throughout the meeting. At one client location, certain attendees felt that they were not required at the workshop and excused themselves. This saved a lot of time for everybody else. If they had stayed, it would have been a huge distraction, and it was not the right use of their time. Everyone appreciated the courage the team members showed to speak up.

Win-Win Agile Games. Trusted teams for improved results.

HELIUM STICK

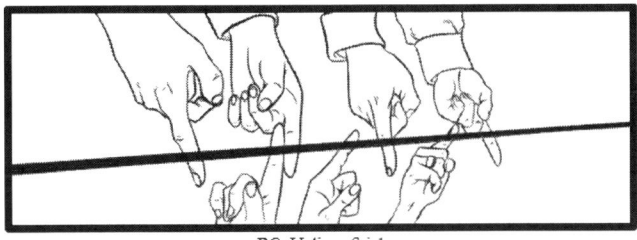

PC: Helium Stick

- **Game Categories:**

| Team Building | Professional Coaching | Retrospectives | Leadership | Others |

- **Game Name:** Helium Stick
- **Objective:** Play this game for team building.
- **Facilitator:** A coach, trainer, or Scrum master.
- **Suggested Attendees:** Product owner and Scrum team(s).
- **Required Materials:** Conference room, helium stick, flip chart, and a timer.
- **Prerequisites:** Logistics planning.
- **Instructions:**
  - ❏ Form groups of eight to twenty people.
  - ❏ Round 1

- ❏ Line up the players in two rows facing each other. Players extend their hands with the index finger pointing out (palms closed, finger-pointed position.)
- ❏ Place the helium stick on the fingers; all fingers must touch the helium stick.
- ❏ The objective is for the players to place the stick in a straight horizontal line by adjusting their fingers. Once the stick is flat, they must collectively bring the stick down to the floor.
- ❏ Teams get a scoring point if they complete the exercise within the allocated time.
- ❏ If a team is unable to put the stick down in a horizontal position, or if any team member's finger is not touching the stick during the exercise, the team must start over.
- ❏ Round 2
  - ❏ Repeat the same exercise.
  - ❏ In this round you may see different results, as the teams have had a chance to practice. Expect teams to perform better.
  - ❏ Debrief on the responses.
- **Timing:**
  - ❏ 15–30 minutes
    - ❏ Round 1: 5 minutes
    - ❏ Debrief: 5 minutes
    - ❏ Round 2: 3 minutes
    - ❏ Debrief: Remaining time

- **Suggested questions for debriefing:**
    - ❏ How did the team feel the first time?
    - ❏ How did team members improve the second time they did the exercise?
    - ❏ Was there a team member who was leading?
    - ❏ What did the group learn?
    - ❏ What solutions did the team discuss for success?
    - ❏ Were there any individual takeaways?

- **Variations:**
    - ❏ Play the game with and without a coach and discuss the pros and cons.

- **Tips and Tricks:**
    - ❏ The Facilitators are encouraged to try variations of this game.

- **Reader Notes:** (Write possible variations and notes below.)
    - ❏ _____
    - ❏ _____
    - ❏ _____

- **Best Time to Play:**

KICK-OFF	PLAN	DO	CHECK	ADJUST
Initiate	*Plan*	*Perform*	*Monitor*	*Improve*

- **Source:** Unknown.

- **Author Notes:** This game heals hearts and is a great team-building activity. It's a go-to game for various formal and informal occasions, but the results are never the same. One memory I have is playing this game with department leaders and their teams. Team members did an outstanding job within their department. When leaders mixed their teams with new team members from another department, the results were mixed (in fact, often not favorable). It took a couple of rounds of playing to get a good debriefing. It was a day of learning for all, including me.

Win-Win Agile Games. Trusted teams for improved results.

HELP! HELP!

PC: Help! Help!

- **Game Categories:**

Team Building	Professional Coaching	Retrospectives	Leadership	Others

- **Game Name:** Help! Help!
- **Objective:** Play this game to foster a safe environment where team members can ask for help.
- **Facilitator:** A coach, trainer, or Scrum master.
- **Suggested Attendees:** Product owner and Scrum team(s).
- **Required Materials:** Conference room, A4 paper, pens, sticky notes, timer, and a flip chart.
- **Prerequisites:** Logistics planning.

- **Instructions:**
  - ❑ Form groups of four to six people.
  - ❑ Each group self-identifies Scrum roles: Product owner, developer, and tester.
  - ❑ Round 1
    - ❑ The Product owner asks the team members to draw a smiley face with their dominant hand using two dots as eyes and a curve as a smile.
    - ❑ Within the allocated time, team members draw as many smileys as they can.
  - ❑ Round 2
    - ❑ The Product owner then asks the team members to draw a smiley face with their nondominant hand using two dots as eyes and a curve as a smile.
    - ❑ Within the allocated time, team members should try to draw as many smileys as they can.
  - ❑ Round 3
    - ❑ The Product owner asks the team to draw a smiley face with their eyes closed. They can use their dominant hand to draw the picture.
    - ❑ If team members open their eyes, they lose a point.
- **Timing:**
  - ❑ 20–45 minutes
    - ❑ Instructions: 3–4 minutes

- ☐ Round 1: 1–3 minutes
- ☐ Round 2: 1–3 minutes
- ☐ Round 3: 1–3 minutes
- ☐ Debrief: Remaining time

- **Suggested questions for debriefing:**
  - ☐ Did anyone ask for the Product owner's help while drawing the picture?
  - ☐ Was there a reason why some team members did not interact with the Product owner much? What was the outcome of teams in this case?
  - ☐ How was the team's experience drawing with closed eyes? Can you relate this scenario to the current project?
  - ☐ Did any team members avoid interacting with other teams because the facilitator did not instruct them to?
  - ☐ Which team successfully drew with another team's help?
  - ☐ What benefits could teams learn by asking for help?

- **Variations:**
  - ☐ Draw variations of the face by adjusting the features.

- **Tips and Tricks:**
  - ☐ The Facilitators are encouraged to try variations of this game.
  - ☐ The facilitator should focus on team members who are hesitating to offer help or ask for help.

- **Reader Notes:** (Write possible variations and notes below.)
  - ☐ _____
  - ☐ _____
  - ☐ _____

- **Best Time to Play:**

KICK-OFF	PLAN	DO	CHECK	ADJUST
Initiate	*Plan*	*Perform*	*Monitor*	*Improve*

- **Source:** Unknown.

- **Author Notes:** One of the key responsibilities as a coach is to work with management to build a safe environment for teams to speak up, to commit, and to deliver. This game brings out various personalities within the team. I played a slight variation of this game with school children. Kids were more open to asking for help during the game. Their goal was to complete the exercise irrespective of who got the credit. Issues were getting resolved quickly. Fast forward: When I facilitated this game in a corporate environment, the results were different. Some attendees were not open to the idea of asking for help. The reasons could have been many, but not opening up resulted in participants' making more assumptions. The team's deliverables were affected, and there was less trust among team members. Although it was just a game, the result was not favorable. Because of a few people, the entire team went down on delivery. The debrief was intense with action items to improve the situation.

REFERENCES

The gaming world is not new. I am not the first writer to write a book about the benefits of games, and I won't be the last. This page is dedicated to all geniuses and predecessors, who have inspired the world already and influenced people like me.

1) [1] "What Is Scrum?" Home | Scrum Guides, https://www.scrumguides.org/

2) Boal, Augusto. Games for Actors and Non-Actors. London: Routledge, 2010

3) Hohmann, Luke. Innovation Games: Creating Breakthrough Products through Collaborative Play. Upper Saddle River, N.J: Addison-Wesley, 2015.

4) Pike, Robert W., and Christopher Busse. 101 Games for Trainers: a Collection of the Best Activities from Creative Training Techniques Newsletter. Amherst, MA: HRD Press, 2004.

5) Thiagarajan, Sivasailam. Thiagis 100 Favorite Games. San Francisco: Pfeiffer, 2006.

6) Boos, Paul, and André Dhondt. TastyCupcakes.org. Accessed September 29, 2019. https://www.tastycupcakes.org

7) Scannell, Mary. The Big Book of Conflict Resolution Games: Quick, Effective Activities to Improve Communication, Trust and Collaboration. New York, NY: McGraw-Hill, 2010.

8) Sweeney, Linda Booth, and Dennis L. Meadows. The Systems Thinking Playbook: Exercises to Stretch and Build Learning and Systems Thinking Capabilities. White River Junction, VT: Chelsea Green Publishing Co, 2013.

9) Alistair Cockburn. Accessed September 29, 2019. https://alistair.cockburn.us

10) Gray, Dave, Sunni Brown, and James Macanufo. Gamestorming: a Playbook for Innovators, Rulebreakers, and Changemakers. Sebastopol, CA: OReilly, 2010.

11) "Tools for Teams and Teamwork." Teampedia. https://www.teampedia.net/wiki/Main_Page

12) Priest, Simon, and Karl Rohnke. 101 Of the Best Corporate Team-Building Activities We Know. Place of publication not identified: TARRAK Technologies, 2000.

13) Wise, Will. Ask Powerful Questions: Create Conversations That Matter. United States: We!, 2017.

14) "Tuckman's Stages of Group Development." Wikipedia. Wikimedia Foundation,

https://en.wikipedia.org/wiki/Tuckman's_stages_of_group_development

15) Fist of five game: https://whatis.techtarget.com/definition/fist-to-five-fist-of-five

16) Rouse, Margaret, and Margaret Rouse. "What Is Fist to Five (Fist of Five)? - Definition from WhatIs.com." WhatIs.com. Accessed September 29, 2019.
https://whatis.techtarget.com/definition/fist-to-five-fist-of-five

17) "Fibonacci Number." Wikipedia. Wikimedia Foundation,
https://en.wikipedia.org/wiki/Fibonacci_number

18) "Why Progressive Estimation Scale Is So Efficient For Teams." Why Progressive Estimation Scale Is So Efficient For Teams.
http://www.yakyma.com/2012/05/why-progressive-estimation-scale-is-so.html

19) "MoSCoW Method." Wikipedia. Wikimedia Foundation,
https://en.wikipedia.org/wiki/MoSCoW_method

20) PC/Illustrations: Savitha Katham / Rafael

And many more who contributed to experimental teaching to address human and corporate needs.

Made in the USA
Middletown, DE
24 January 2020